Hope for the Weary Mom

STACEY THACKER   BROOKE MCGLOTHLIN

HARVEST HOUSE PUBLISHERS
EUGENE, OREGON

Cover by Knail, Salem, Oregon

Cover photo © Shutterstock / Kite_rin

Stacey Thacker and Brooke McGlothlin are represented by MacGregor Literary, Inc.

All the incidents described in this book are true. Where individuals may be identifiable, they have granted the author and the publisher the right to use their names, stories, and/or facts of their lives in all manners, including composite or altered representations. In all other cases, names, circumstances, descriptions, and details have been changed to render individuals unidentifiable.

HOPE FOR THE WEARY MOM

Copyright © 2012 by Stacey Thacker and Brooke McGlothlin
Published by Harvest House Publishers
Eugene, Oregon 97402
www.harvesthousepublishers.com

Library of Congress Cataloging-in-Publication Data
    Thacker, Stacey, 1971-
    Hope for the weary mom / Stacey Thacker and Brooke McGlothlin.
        pages cm
    Includes bibliographical references.
    ISBN 978-0-7369-6080-9 (pbk.)
    ISBN 978-0-7369-6081-6 (eBook)
    1. Mothers—Religious life. 2. Motherhood—Religious aspects—Christianity. I. Title.
    BV4529.18.T444 2015
    248.8'431—dc23
                                                                2014020269

Contents

For the weary mom buried underneath
the mess of life and believes she is alone.
You are not. Hope is here.
Let's walk together.

Acknowledgments

Stacey

Mike: Thank you for your love, support, and believing I am a writer. I could not have done this without your support. Thanks for helping to make my dream come true.

My girls: I am the most blessed mom in the world to have you as daughters. Thanks for cheering for mommy and for giving me time to write each day. You are awesome and I love you very much.

Mom: We have learned this year that hope is the anchor that holds us in all things. I love you so much and am proud to be the daughter of such a brave woman.

Dad: You have seen face to face what we only see dimly now. I'm so glad we have the hope of heaven and eternity together. I miss you every day.

Robin, Angie, Tanya, Krystal, Emily, and Gretchen: Thank you for taking the time to read rough chapters and for encouraging me. I was able to trust you with my heart on the page because you are more like sisters than friends.

Kristin: Thank you for listening to the Lord and for seeing what "Hope" could be. Your love and support mean the world to us.

Brooke: I can't believe I get to be on this journey with you. I love seeing Jesus shine through your words and ministry. You are a gift to me, sweet friend.

Chip: Thank you for believing in "Hope" and finding the perfect home for it. I am truly grateful for your support and hard work.

Kathleen and the Harvest House Publishers Team: Thank you for saying yes and giving us a chance to reach even more moms with "Hope." It has been an honor partnering with you!

Jesus: Thank you for seeing me in my mess and meeting me in the broken place. You loved me too much to leave me there, and called me out into a place of "Hope." May you be glorified through this humble offering and touch every heart who reads it.

Brooke

Cory: Thank you for just doing. For cleaning, washing, bathing, feeding, teaching, and all of the other things you did so I could have time to write. You're a gift to me.

Boys: You're the reason for this book, but even on the hardest days I'm still so very thankful that I get to be your mama. Thank you for keeping me desperate for Jesus, and for always giving me big, squishy boy hugs when I need them. You're my favorite boys in the world!

Mom and Dad: You've always believed in my dreams. Now, as an adult, I can clearly see that you've not only believed in my dreams, but sacrificed for them as well. I can only hope to love my children so well. Thank you for cutting your trip to Florida short to come home so I could have time to finish this book. I couldn't have done it without you.

Jamie and Meggen: Thank you so much for cheering me on, encouraging me to keep going, and for the way you have served me throughout the last difficult season of my life. I won't forget.

Kristin: You listened to the Lord. Thank you.

Tracey Lane: Thank you for letting me into your heart and for talking so freely about Jarrett. I'm privileged to have known him.

Stacey: I can't imagine writing this book with anyone else. If I had to be "stuck" with someone, I'm sure glad it was you! I'm so grateful for your words of advice and encouragement, both in this book and in my life.

Erin Mohring, Jamie Soranno, and Logan Wolfram: Thank you for helping me brainstorm Mommy strengths and for sharing your stories.

Chip MacGregor: You believed in us and in the need to keep reaching out to weary moms. Thank you for catching the vision and for championing it for us in ways that went above and beyond the call of duty. We're so grateful for you.

Lysa TerKeurst: You have been such a gift. Thank you for your encouragement, wisdom, and expert input on this manuscript. We're grateful for you and the ministry of Compel.

The Hope for the Weary Mom launch team: No words really cut it. Thank you for your faithful prayers, feedback, and encouragement to get this message out. You are grace to us.

My Jesus: You're enough.

From One Weary Mom to Another

*Y*ou'd think that because I've written a few books for parents and, oh, about a gazillion parenting articles and blogs I'd have this mothering thing down. I've been a mom for a while, so that should help too. The truth is, at the time I'm writing this my kids are ages 24, 21, 19, 6, 3, and 3. And I'm weary. WEARY.

I get a lot of responses when I tell people that I'm a mom of six children. And then when I tell their ages people really get confused. After raising our three oldest children almost to adulthood, God led John and me to adopt three more. We adopted Alyssa (one of the three-year-olds) at birth, and just last year we adopted Bella (six), and Casey (three) from the foster care system. To be completely honest I thought it would be easier the second time around. I learned how to set priorities and to focus on what's truly important while not trying to compare myself to others. After raising three kids—the feeding and fretting, bathing and battling, caring and correcting—you'd think I'd have this mom thing figured out. (Or at least that's what I thought.) Wrong!

I do have a few more tricks up my sleeve, and I've taken a major chill pill (or maybe it's just softening with age), but parenting is still HARD. There are times I'm trying to bathe a cranky preschooler or discipline two children who are at each other's throats, and I wonder, "Why did I sign up for this again?" There are moments when I hear "Mommy!" from the other room and I'd rather pull the covers over my head than get up and make a sausage biscuit. (I'm pretty sure my three-year-old boy eats sausage for breakfast every morning. "Sausage" was his first word!)

I get weary of power struggles, of putting my needs last, of trying to remember important things like making healthy meals, keeping electrical outlets plugged, and reading Bible stories in order to plant God's Word in my kids' hearts. And it's not that I've stopped my mothering role with the bigger ones either. They need advice, clean laundry, and college essays previewed, but mostly they need a listening ear. They need someone to be outraged about their unrealistic Western Civilizations professor as much as they are. They need someone to ask, "What's wrong?" when it's obvious that something is. And as my oldest has become a parent himself, he needs advice on his parenting—which I only try to give when I'm asked!

Parenting is more work than I ever dreamed of. With kids on both ends of the spectrum I realize this afresh on a daily basis. Thankfully, I have God to turn to. He is my strength, my wisdom, and my hope. Thankfully, there are books like *Hope for the Weary Mom* that remind me I'm not alone. That point me in the right direction…but mostly point me back to God.

Feeling frazzled, overwhelmed, unappreciated, and downright weary? Well, you've come to the right book. Brooke and Stacey are moms who are walking this road too, and who are here to stretch their invisible arms through these pages to offer you a hug of understanding…and some pretty amazing advice too!

I know these women, and I know their hearts for moms. These pages have been bathed in prayer even as they've been filled with God's Truth. Know that you, reader, have been prayed for. Know that you aren't alone. Know that there is Someone who will be there for you during your weary moments. And be encouraged as Brooke and Stacey share their own journey to finding strength and peace from the One who loves them most—the One, Jesus, who loves you most too.

Walking the weary (but joyful) road with you,

Tricia Goyer

author of more than 40 books, including
Blue Like Play Dough: The Shape of Motherhood in the Grip of God
www.triciagoyer.com

Introduction

Dear Weary Mom,

If you are reading this a couple of things may be true of you. First, you are a mom. Second, you are weary, tired, and waving the white flag. You also may have seen the word hope and thought, "I could use some of that tossed my way."

In 2011, I poured out my heart in a blog post called, "Steve Jobs, Me, and Being Fresh Out of Amazing." Here is what it said:

> So the big news this week is that Steve Jobs has resigned as CEO of Apple. In a letter to the Apple Board and Community he said:
>
> "I have always said if there ever came a day when I could no longer meet my duties and expectations as Apple's CEO, I would be the first to let you know. Unfortunately, that day has come."[1]
>
> As I read this I had one thought: What happens when you are a mom, and you feel like you are not meeting your duties or the expectations of others and you can't step down? Who do you let know?
>
> Here's the letter I would write if I had somewhere to send it:
>
> Dear Lord, (I figured I should go straight to the top)
>
> I have always said (well, lately anyway) that if I could no

11

longer meet my duties and expectations as a wife, mom, teacher, and cheerleader to the five others living in this house, I would let you know. Today, that day has come. I have...

- yelled
- screamed (is that the same thing?)
- cried
- asked forgiveness
- yelled
- screamed
- cried
- and, well, you get the picture.

I've pretty much fallen short in every category. I am tired and not really good for much right now. The trouble is, Lord, that I need to be amazing and I'm fresh out of amazing. At least it sure feels that way.

Lord, I'm dry. Empty. Hit the wall. I got nothing. I just thought I'd let you know. But then again, You already do."O Lord, you have examined my heart and know everything about me" (Psalm 139:1).

So, friend, can you relate to this? It is okay if you can't; you can just pray for me or send chocolate. I so wish we could have this chat at Starbucks over coffee.[2]

To my surprise, the response from other moms was significant. Many moms commented that they could relate to my struggle.

My friend Brooke was one of these moms. She said, "I can so relate to what you're saying here, Stacey, because I feel the same way. Right now, I've got nothing to give. Nothing. Nada. I'm tired and don't feel well and honestly, I want a break from everything." I responded to her comment. She later emailed me to continue our discussion. From this conversation, *Hope for the Weary Mom* was born.

Brooke and I realized we were not alone in the weariness. We wanted to find a way to encourage other moms who are like us, sitting at home in their kitchens feeling the same way, so we wrote a few blog posts, established a website, created a Facebook page and Twitter hashtag (#WearyMom) because we are bloggers and that is what we do.

We took a chance and put the *Hope for the Weary Mom* blog series into a tiny little e-book and offered it for free to the subscribers of two of our blogs, *Mothers of Daughters* and *The MOB Society* (for mothers of boys). We also made it available for Kindle readers on Amazon for a small fee. In the process we found thousands of other moms who were looking for a little hope, too. God's plans for *Hope* were so much bigger than we had imagined. Over the next few months, we were astounded by the response to the message.

Brooke and I will tell you we don't have this all figured out. This journey is our journey. *Hope for the Weary Mom* has become more than a blog post or the book you are holding in your hand. It is now our passion to encourage every mom who is overwhelmed by the weariness of life with the truth that God sees her—that He wants to meet her in the middle of her mess and offer her true and lasting Hope.

Please know that we are so glad you are taking this journey of *Hope* with us. We are praying for you.

Let's move on with Hope.

Stacey Thacker
Brooke McGlothlin

Chapter 1

When Your Weakness
Is All You Can See

Brooke

Beer and cigarettes.

Yep…you read that right. Beer and cigarettes. The phone call went something like this:

"Honey, I need you to come home now. The two-year-old is screaming because he wants to sit on my lap while I'm nursing the baby. The baby is screaming because the two-year-old keeps trying to sit on his head. When the two-year-old tries to sit on the baby's head he can't nurse. Now he won't nurse at all and is screaming his head off. The bulldog has started crying because he wants to be fed (doesn't everybody!!) and I'm going to explode within the next ten minutes if you don't COME HOME AND BRING ME BEER AND CIGARETTES RIGHT NOW!"

He brought me a Coke and dark chocolate.

Super-Sonic Weaknesses

My precious boys were born just 23 months apart. We didn't necessarily plan it that way, but it happened nonetheless. If you've read my book *Praying for Boys: Asking God for the Things They Need Most*, you'll know that I actually prayed and asked God to give us boys! I wanted to raise men who loved the Lord with all of their hearts, who

15

would choose to take a stand for what's right, who would be world-changers. It had occurred to me that there was a shortage of truly godly men in the world, and that as parents, we were losing the battle for the hearts of our sons. So during a time of self-righteous pride in my own ability as a mother (yes...this was *before* we had kids) I asked God to give us boys. And he indulged me.

My boys, like any number of other little boys in the world, are infatuated with being superheroes. My life as a mother of boys includes masks, swords, light sabers, and dueling bad guys to the death.

There's rarely a day that goes by in the McGlothlin Home for Boys that doesn't involve someone wearing a cape.

I love it. I hope they always want to rescue damsels in distress, bring flowers to their mommy, and fight bad guys. Pretending to rescue those who are weaker makes them feel useful and important. Running around our house with their capes flapping in the wind makes them feel strong. I believe developing these characteristics in young boys sets them up for strength, compassion, and boldness later in life. Superheroes, those found on television, in storybooks, and (the best ones!) in the Bible give my boys something to pattern their lives after. And that's very, very good.

Yes, I want to raise strong boys. But most of the time, I have to confess, I feel terribly weak.

During that first year of my little guy's life there were many nights I didn't think we were going to make it. Both of our boys are "those boys." You know, the ones who are extremely high energy, get into everything, don't take no for an answer, would rather wrestle than breathe, only have one volume (LOUD), and generally leave my husband and me completely breathless at the end of the day? Even as little guys they fought a lot, and they still bicker more often than not.

My inner voice, the one that likes to show me all my ugly, had a field day telling me I would never measure up as a mom.

Sound familiar?

The night I called my husband asking for beer and cigarettes I was in a state of panic. I'm not a beer drinker, and I only smoked a few times in college (sorry, Mom and Dad). But as I sat on my front stoop in tears that night, cell phone in hand, toddler in the Pack 'n Play, baby in the swing (and the stinking bulldog tied to the chair!), something in me snapped. After months of trying so hard to put on a brave and sure face to my friends and family, I broke down and admitted there was no way I could raise these boys by myself.

Now maybe you're stronger than I am. Maybe you're one of those moms who has it all together. Your children jump to attention at your every command, are polite to strangers, and dance a jig while they do their chores. Maybe you don't scare the neighbors by yelling, "HELP ME, JESUS!!!" at the top of your lungs multiple times a day.

But I do. And I bet if you're honest, your life isn't all peaches and cream either. (If it is, you need to be the one writing this book!)

Of course, things do change as they grow up. It's been six years since that episode on my front porch, and I don't have anyone tugging on me to nurse or trying to sit on a sibling's head anymore (okay…maybe sometimes). We lost our precious bulldog to cancer and now have two energetic lab puppies. But I still have incredibly active, highly distractible, in-your-face little boys. Sometimes I'm tempted to think I'm all alone in my walk, and those days threaten to overwhelm me. My complete inability to change their hearts of stone into hearts of flesh makes my weaknesses blaze until they're all I can see.

We moms, we think we're all alone, don't we? We think our problems are worse than everyone else's. We think our children's sinful hearts are more sinful than everyone else's. We think our weak spots have to be hidden and can't imagine telling the truth about what's happening in our hearts. Maybe it sounds a little like this…

I've dreaded this day for over a week. Cautiously, I peek my head around the corner, just barely daring to poke it inside the door, and see that my worst fears have come true. Spotted, greeted by the mother of the birthday boy, I have no time to tuck tail and run, so I muster up all the courage I have, walk in the room, and find myself face-to-face with the non-crafty mom's worst nightmare:

The crafty-mom birthday party (cue Stephen King-ish music and the obligatory don, don, doooooooonnnnnnn).

The room is one big science experiment, literally. My friend Danielle has spent weeks preparing for the little boy birthday party of the century, and it shows. Green slime taunts me. Carefully crafted explosions that make little boys squeal with delight mock me. The entire table of elements taped above a table filled with edible petri dishes stares me down and makes me want to run and hide.

I look for a means of escape, but the exits are blocked by innocent bystanders. Wait, there's an open window. If I grab the boys by the shirt collar and quietly stuff them out the window we can shimmy down the drain pipe to the playground below and no one will know we're gone. Shoot, now they're making liquid ice on the other side of the room. New plan.

Maybe I can bribe them away. That's it. I'll woo them with the promise of a trip to Dairy Queen for their favorite ice cream before the cake is served. What's that? Hot dogs? Man! Because of our new healthy eating plan they haven't had one in a month. I'll never get them away now. They're going to figure out my big secret any second now...Mama is the most un-crafty person in the world, and birthday parties stress me out like nothing else. I'd hoped they would never see "the other side." That they would never know a birthday party could be anything other than a trip to the pool with all their friends.

Busted.

I sit down in a collapsible chair, thinking about how my own birthday party facade is collapsing bit by bit when it happens. Those big, brown eyes that make it oh-so-difficult to stay mad for long look up at me...and he says it. Oh glory, the one thing that makes me just want to end it all, give up trying, hire a professional...anything to ease this feeling of complete and utter failure.

"Mom, why can't our birthday parties be more like this one?"
Sigh.

Every summer the "I'm not good enough" feelings start to creep in and make me want to give up even trying to plan a good party for my boys. Thankfully, in God's great and infinite mercy, He allowed my boys' birthdays to be just three weeks apart. They've never known individual birthday parties, and I plan to ride that wave until it spits me out on the beach, ragged and torn. The fact of the matter is that I don't have a crafty bone in my body, and it never shows more than when I'm planning a birthday party.

I hate sewing.

I don't own a glue gun.

I couldn't tell you where the tape is.

Our glue sticks are all dried out.

My boys bribe the neighbor's little girl to let them use her scissors and duct tape. And I've actually considered hiring her to do craft time with my boys once a week after she gets home from school.

My lack of crafting ability has grown my stress level to epic proportions, and my feelings of guilt and utter failure have grown with it.

One recent Thanksgiving I decided to force myself out of my non-crafty comfort zone and tried to prepare a day of wonderful education and hands-on experience for my boys. As a homeschooling family, we're always looking for ways to make the calendar come alive, and it had occurred to me that my boys, then six and four, had never really learned the story of Thanksgiving. I decided it was time for that to change.

I spent hours at my local bookstore picking out just the right books to communicate the message of Thanksgiving I wanted them to remember. I scoured the Internet looking for an audio book of the story of Squanto because my oldest loves learning about Native Americans. I painstakingly cut a Thanksgiving Tree from brown craft paper and decorated its branches with colored leaves made from outlines of my precious sons' hands, each one marked with something they were thankful for that day.

It was shaping up to be a wonderful success. That Thanksgiving Tree was my crowning crafty achievement, my very heart and soul hanging there on the wall. It should have been the best Thanksgiving ever...except it wasn't.

In reality, I spent most of Thanksgiving Day sobbing—and possibly slightly hysterical—because I couldn't believe my sons could still be so selfish, ungrateful, and yes, *thankless,* after all I'd done to serve them throughout the month. They were disobedient, ugly, unkind, and downright mean all day long, and it made me feel a bit like throwing something. I mean, couldn't they see how my hands shook as I cut that craft paper into a tree? Couldn't they see the look of sheer uncrafty determination in my eyes as I traced their little hands and taped them to the wall each day?

I may have yelled. And screamed. And wept. And threatened. And shaken with anger over their petty arguments that were making our "celebration" a smashing...well...failure. I felt beaten down by their attitudes, and at one point literally curled away from everyone in the passenger seat of our SUV in something reminiscent of the fetal position. The words going through my mind?

This will never change. I just don't have what it takes to be the mom they need. I'm a crafting failure so I must be a failure as a mom.

I should just quit trying.

Glorified Weaknesses

So be honest, mom. How many times since you brought those blue or pink bundles home from the hospital have you just wanted to quit trying? Maybe it's something much more serious than crafting that makes you want to give up. I struggle with yelling. I get angry too often. I like things to go my way, and when they don't I can make everyone in my life miserable. Your areas of weakness could be totally different, but I bet if I asked you to list them right now you could spout them off one by one. Am I right?

How many times a day do you catch yourself thinking about

what a failure you are, or how your one big mess-up will probably land that little person who watches everything you do straight in the counseling chair a bit later in life? How much of your day do you spend glorifying your weaknesses (dwelling on them, allowing negative internal commentary about them to beat you down, thinking about them constantly, etc.) and wondering what will happen if everybody finds out the truth about who you *really* are?

Glorifying weaknesses—no matter how big or small—sucks our souls dry of the life-giving hope we need to just keep going.

But there is a different way. I'm convinced that the place of our greatest weakness can unleash the power of God's greatest grace. Instead of glorifying our weaknesses, letting them control our lives and break our hearts, we can learn to use them to glorify God, confessing our weaknesses and trusting him to make them into something good.

It was during a phone call with a friend that I finally decided I might not be the only one with these kinds of issues. We'd been chatting about church this and that for just a few seconds when she interrupted the conversation to tell the little voice in her home to stop what he was doing. When that same little voice turned a bit nasty and screamed, "NO I WON'T!" to his mama on the phone, a lightbulb went off in my heart, and I knew I'd met a kindred spirit…or at least another human being who knew what I was going through.

It was a profound moment for me, inspiring me to step out from behind the curtains of my life into the light. One phone call empowered me to connect with other mothers of boys and tell my ugly truth, because I suddenly knew that if I felt alone and desperate in my mothering—consumed with the way my weaknesses were affecting my boys—there had to be other moms who felt the same way. Soon after that simple phone conversation, the Lord placed a dream in my heart for what would eventually become the MOB (Mothers of Boys) Society—an online, Christian community helping mothers delight in the chaos of raising boys. A place where boy moms can feel safe, let it all hang out, and find community and help around raising these wild and crazy, beautiful and boisterous, overwhelming but amazing boys.

I chose a piece of truth that can only be found in community.

I chose to fill the empty spaces of a weary mom's life with truth instead of complaining, faith instead of fretting, grace instead of comparison, and yes...coke and dark chocolate instead of beer and cigarettes.

The place of our greatest weakness can unleash the power of God's greatest grace.

I stopped listening to the voices that pointed out my shame and beat me down and started filling my heart with the voice of truth.

It all sounds simple when you read it now, but in reality it can take a while to make God's voice of truth the one you hear in your moments of great weakness. Second Corinthians 12:9-10, verses that have become some of the most important, inspiring truths of my life, says it this way:

> But he said to me, "My grace is sufficient for you, for my power is made perfect in weakness." Therefore I will boast all the more gladly of my weaknesses, so that the power of Christ may rest upon me. For the sake of Christ, then, I am content with weaknesses, insults, hardships, persecutions, and calamities. For when I am weak, then I am strong.

I imagine that if Jesus himself could whisper these verses into our hearts it might sound something like this:

Can you hear me, sweet one? I'm struggling hard to be heard over the condemning voices in your head, but I want you to hear the truth and embrace it. It's okay to be weak. It's okay to not know what to do or how to do it. It's okay that you don't have the answers. I do.

What's that? You're tuning in just a little now? I'll try again…It's okay to feel lost. It's okay to need help. It's okay that you're not perfect. I am!

That's better! You're the apple of my eye! My darling girl who was so valuable to me that I gave my life for you! I want to shout my love for you from the rooftops and say it's okay to fail! It's okay to get things wrong! IT'S OKAY TO BE WEAK, because in your weakness I AM strong.

If you'll let me, I will make your place of greatest weakness into my place of greatest grace. I'll be the strength you need to keep going, the one who meets you in your mess, the one who leads you to the next right thing and covers over your sin with my robe of righteousness. Trust me. Invite me in. Shut out those other voices, because I have loved you with an everlasting love. Nothing can ever tear you away from the strength of my love. Listen to me.

Whatever strengths and weaknesses we possess are all a part of God's plan for our beautiful, messy lives. He uses every detail of our mess for his greater glory, and can redeem even our deepest, darkest, most daring mistakes until they're more beautiful than we could've ever imagined.

My friend Jess came to Christ in her late thirties. Prior to this, she led something of a double life—taking the moral high ground during the day, and struggling with promiscuity, pornography, and other sinful, damaging choices by night. At times paralyzed by depression and anxiety, she was crumbling from the inside out.

Desperate for relief, Jess found herself in the office of a Christian counselor. She tells her story like this: "Two things moved me forward during that time. First, the threat of being hospitalized. That scared me to death. Second, my counselor shared Philippians 4:13 with me, which says, 'I can do all things through him who strengthens me.' She also prayed for me during each of our sessions. No one had ever done that. Besides rote prayer and rosaries, I didn't know how to pray. And to be honest, I had given up on prayer except in times of great need when I'd simply promise God that I'd change my lifestyle, my behavior, anything, if only he'd take away the hurt. Medication, counseling, and clinging for dear life to the one Bible verse I knew by heart slowly enabled me to begin moving forward. And then God brought me my husband, Ed. I got pregnant rather quickly and spent a lot of time in prayer. Fear of my old sinful life-style catching up with me somehow or affecting our child scared me to death. I was filled with deep guilt and horrible shame. After years of actually blocking many incidents out, they came flooding back. At the time I thought it was due to all the hormones. Now I see that God wanted me to deal with them. I was driving to work one morning and, as was my habit, talking to my unborn daugh-ter. I also liked to sing to her, so I turned on the radio. I was flipping through unfamiliar Montana radio stations when I heard Michael W. Smith's voice. I recognized it from my college days, but it was a new song. I had never heard it before.

"But the chorus suddenly blared from my not-so-loud volume setting. I heard it loud and clear. I got it. I received it. And for the first time in my entire life, I believed it. At that moment, my life changed. It was never the same. I finally knew I was forgiven. JESUS CHRIST had died for me. ME! Now, I'm able to share my testi-mony of amazing grace with those God puts in my life. I know that if God can redeem the worst in me, he can do it for others, too. I could never have made these changes in my life alone. So you see, it's all him. I'm thrilled to tell others about what I'm not so they can clearly see what he is."

The thing I love most about Jess's story is that last sentence. "I'm thrilled to tell others about what I'm not so they can clearly see what he is." It's what 2 Corinthians 12:9-10 calls "boasting in weakness," and it's the very best way to see God be strong in your life.

So boast, Mom. Boast in the fact that you're not good enough, not strong enough, not smart enough, *not enough* to be a good mom, and watch what God does. That's right, boast. Tell the world you don't have it all together, don't always know the right thing to do, and don't have all the answers. Admit that your kids sometimes have fistfights or shove each other off the new toy. Own up to the yelling and wiggle out of the straitjacket you've been wearing, bound up by a need to be perfect.

Refuse those voices that cry out, "Failure! Mother mess-up!" and instead take them straight to Jesus. Even if they're true—especially if they're true—take them straight to the one who loves you and invite him in, trusting him to make his strength perfect in your weakness.

Boast in your weakness, and then be truly strong.

Chapter 2

When You're Caught in What You're Not

Brooke

In the last chapter, we talked about how our weaknesses can be the place of God's greatest grace—that intersection of our lack and God's strength—where He takes our mess and makes it beautiful. But when your weakness is all you can see, it's important to remember that you've been created with certain God-given strengths, too.

Had you forgotten about those, Mom? I know I did. For several years, as I entrenched myself deeper and deeper in the world of mommyhood, I forgot that God had created me to be good at certain things and that he wanted me to use them for his glory. If I'm honest, there were times I wondered if I was still supposed to be pouring into my gifts while my kids were young, or if I should just totally put aside the things that make me light up on the inside, waiting to use them for another time.

More often, though, I struggled to see myself clearly. It was like looking in a mirror covered with the newspaper clippings of all my failures in big, bold, print and squinting to see behind them, looking for an accurate reflection of the woman God created me to be.

It's just easier to see the things we're not good at. I've already shared how I'm no good at crafting. Maybe you're a terrible cook.

Maybe you struggle to engage your children in meaningful conversation. Maybe you're just not all that organized, or you often find yourself forgetting important things that other moms seem to easily remember. Whatever the case, I bet at some point you've squinted into the mirror too, trying to figure out who that woman looking back at you through the black and white stamps of your failures really was.

Not Enough or Just Too Much

As I've watched women over the years and studied the characteristics of human behavior in my counseling studies, I've seen some patterns emerge based on the qualities of our God-given personalities. For example, I'm an introvert, so people don't energize me. That doesn't mean I don't love people, or can't be around them. (I'm a speaker for goodness' sake.) It just means that when I need to be energized, I do it best alone.

During a difficult time in my life, Stacey asked me what I do to push through the stress and keep going. Without even thinking twice I replied, "I have to get alone, get in the Word, and pray until God meets me and gives me the strength I need to get back up and move again." Being alone energizes me.

I've often thought that one of the perks of having a husband who works shift-work—at least for me—is that I get a lot of time alone. When he's working evenings, I can put the boys to bed and still have two or three hours to myself. I go to bed those nights feeling refreshed and ready for the next day. But when I don't get enough alone time, or when I'm forced to do things outside of my introverted comfort zone for too long, I can get fussy or start zoning out.

In addition to being an introvert, I'm also a relater. That may sound crazy based on what I just described, but I find that most people are either *relaters* or *doers*. Relaters tend to be better communicators than workers. (Not that communication isn't work; it is. And not that working doesn't require communication skills; it does.

I'll explain this more in just a minute!) For example, I'm much better at coming up with goals than implementing them. I excel at communicating on a heart level with people, but I struggle to be the fun mom who heads up the T-ball snack schedule. I'm a visionary for the MOB Society, always dreaming up new ways to reach the hearts of mothers of boys, but I need people to come alongside me to get the job done so my dreams don't fizzle out.

Because I'm an introverted relater, I tend to feel more secure in small groups. I've never been one of those girls who thrived in large groups of friends. Like Anne of Green Gables, I much prefer one or two "bosom friends." One-on-one friendships, or maybe at the most two or three, give me the safety I need to share my heart. I can speak to a group of 500 women and be fine because the collective group feels like one woman. But when I have to go down offstage and mingle, sharing my heart and interacting with a lot of people at one time, it's much harder. Over the years I've learned that I can push myself to do it anyway for the sake of building relationships and ministering to the women I'm speaking to, but it takes all the creative energy I have. After it's over, you can bet I'll be shutting down, curling up with a book, or putting in my headphones to get some good, rejuvenating me-time. If I don't, I can't function.

This affects my time with my boys, too. They're loud (as I've mentioned, you know, just a few times), and want to be with me all the time. Well, really, not just with me…they want to be *on* me. Face to face, spitting on my glasses, elbows poking me in the ribs, and hands messing up my hair. I know there will be a day when I'll miss that, but right now it makes for one depleted mama and leaves me without a whole lot of energy left over for other things.

Honestly, I'd really like to be the mom who's ready to wrestle, play, and be crafty with her boys all day long. I'd like to naturally be the mom who loves having large groups of boys over to her house so they can burp and fart while she feeds them large quantities of food. But I'm not.

For the sake of my boys, I do these things from time to time. I've been known to wrestle until something gets broken, and I try to have my boys' friends over often enough to get to know them well. As they get older, my husband and I will commit to making our home a safe place for our boys and their friends—meaning some of my precious quiet time will fly out the window—but I've come to the conclusion that it's never going to be comfortable for me to do it. I will always excel in smaller numbers, and I'll always need plenty of time to recuperate when I can't get them.

As moms, it's easy to look at our lack and get depressed about all the things we don't naturally bring to the table for our kids. Too many times I've looked with longing at my fun mom friends and envied the way they capture their children's hearts. Maybe that's why I tried to keep the crafty mom birthday parties away from my kids for so long. I look at the fun mom and I see my lack. More than that, I look at the fun mom and think my kids are going to love her more than they love me. What does it matter if I can reach their hearts in the tough times if another mom already has their hearts captured through her fun, bubbly personality?

Wishing to be something we're not is enough to drive a mama mad with envy and frustration! But I've found that the best cure for a mom who's caught in what she's not is to focus on what she's got.

When you're caught in what you're not,
focus on what you've got.

God-Given Strengths

As I look at the lives of the moms around me, I often see patterns such as the ones I described above emerge from their day-to-day lives. The things that lie outside of our normal, God-given strengths—like me preferring small groups to large, noisy ones—somehow make us feel that we're a failure at life…at being moms.

The truth is I'm just not at my best in loud, crazy, large-group situations and I don't have a crafty bone in my body. When I'm faced with other moms who are really getting it right in these areas, I'm sometimes left feeling like I have to change who I am—who God made me to be—just to keep up. If I let myself dwell on it for too long, I'm left feeling like I'll never measure up in this particular area, or any other area.

Isn't it amazing how one area of weakness can make us feel like we're failing at everything? I think the devil has a field day with our "I'm failing at motherhood" emotions. But what if *not* measuring up in every area was okay? What if we all started measuring our success as mothers based on our areas of innate strength instead of weakness and trusted God enough to fill in the gaps?

We all have God-given gifts and talents—things we're good at just because God made us that way. My friend Jamie is an amazing servant. Somehow, she knows what our family needs before I even tell her what's going on! She may twitch a little when forced outside of her routine, but her natural bent toward encouragement is surpassed by none. My friend Erin is a great connector of people, and her bubbly personality puts everyone at ease. She worries sometimes that people think she's flighty, but her gracious and kind heart make her easy to love. And my friend Logan is a girl who knows how to get things done! Terribly efficient, with a larger-than-life personality, she's a natural on the stage. She may have to learn the art of saying "no" to people, but she's a master at delegating to get things done!

See what I mean?

Focus on What You've Got

Because of my counseling background, I tend to see people fitting nicely into the categories of Relaters and Doers, Extroverts and

Introverts. When we mesh these categories together, we get a nice little chart that looks something like this:

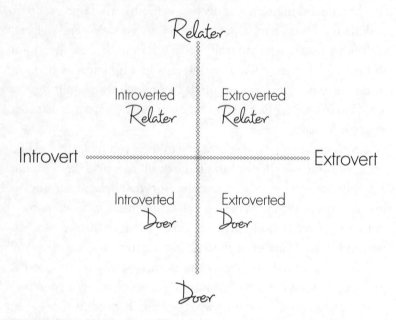

The cross-sections of this chart allow us to more deeply understand our strengths and weaknesses, and they give us four clear categories into which *most* women fall: Introverted Doers, Introverted Relaters, Extroverted Doers, and Extroverted Relaters. (Please note: These categories aren't meant to be exclusive. You might see a little piece of yourself in all of them, but there should be one that's *most* like you).

Introverts vs. Extroverts

To help us get started, allow me to establish some definitions of these terms. According to Susan Cain, author of *Quiet: The Power of Introverts in a World That Can't Stop Talking*, introverts and extroverts differ in the level of outside stimulation they require to function well.

Introverts feel "just right" with less stimulation, as when they sip wine with a close friend, solve a crossword puzzle, or read a book. Extroverts enjoy the extra bang that comes from activities like meeting new people, skiing slippery slopes, and cranking up the stereo. Extroverts are the people who will add life to your dinner party and laugh generously at your jokes. They tend to be assertive, dominant, and in great need of company. Extroverts think out loud and on their feet; they prefer talking to listening, rarely find themselves at a loss for words, and occasionally blurt out things they never meant to say. Introverts…may have strong social skills and enjoy parties and business meetings, but after a while wish they were home in their pajamas. They prefer to devote their social energies to close friends, colleagues, and family. They listen more than they talk, think before they speak, and often feel as if they express themselves better in writing than in conversation.[1]

Some studies suggest that the difference between introverts and extroverts has less to do with how they function in social situations (although that can clearly be a part of the equation) and more on how they recharge afterward. I've already described how that's a big part of my own personal experience of what it means to be an introvert, so for our purposes, we'll use the following definitions:

Introvert: Someone who feels safer and more comfortable functioning one on one or in very small groups and who must recharge alone after long periods of close contact in large groups.

Specific Weakness: Requires long periods of alone time to function well.

Specific Strength: Able to develop very strong relationships with a select few people, thereby reaching deeper into the lives of the people they know well.

Extrovert: Someone who feels energized by large groups, new and exciting experiences, and is often described as "the life of the party."

Specific Weakness: In spite of having lots of acquaintances, the extrovert may feel lonely from the tendency to have broad rather than deep relationships.

Specific Strength: Able to have influence over large numbers of people, thereby reaching a broader audience, affecting the lives of many instead of just a few.

Doers vs. Relaters

I mentioned before that I consider myself a Relater—someone who is good at getting to the heart of the matter with others. Relaters tend to be good at leading people into deeper conversations. I'm not much for small talk, although I've learned to do it over the years, and I just seem programmed to draw people out of their shell and bring the conversation to the level of the heart. Relaters serve others by helping them understand themselves better.

My mother-in-law, on the other hand, is a committed doer. If I can be counted on to say the right things, she can be counted on to do the right things. In the winter of 2014, my husband had his ACL repaired. One morning soon after the surgery, my mother-in-law called to check on his progress. Totally off the cuff, he told her he wished we had invested in a recliner so he could get off the couch a little. The first 72 hours post-op were somewhat grueling for us all, and by the morning of the third day, his back had begun to hurt from not being able to move.

It was a Saturday, so we did our normal Saturday stuff—cleaning house, doing laundry, and just hanging out. My husband couldn't really go anywhere (or even get off the couch without help), so I had spent more time than usual cleaning our glass doors, dusting, and getting down on my hands and knees to vacuum up the dog hair in the cracks and crevices of our home. As it turns out, that was a brilliant thing to do—one always wants her home to be dog hair free when her mother-in-law shows up with a brand new recliner! Yes, the wonderful woman who raised my husband heard the need in her son's voice and just made it happen. We would never have gone out and purchased a new recliner, and as it turned out, just having it made a world of difference in my husband's recovery.

That story (which blessed our socks off…truly) sums up what a doer really is—someone who serves others by working on their behalf, often behind the scenes.

So why is all this important? Because where we fall on the chart above—as an Extroverted Relater, an Extroverted Doer, an Introverted Relater, or an Introverted Doer—does much to define our feelings of success or failure as a mother, and maybe more importantly, as a person. There are key things women in these categories tend to think and say about their strengths and weaknesses, and while the following categories aren't exclusive (in other words, you might see parts of yourself in categories other than your main one), they do tend to describe most people. Unfortunately, we tend to emphasize our weaknesses and forget to see the way God made us as beautiful and a gift to others around us. Let's explore that a bit now.

The Introverted Relater

Introverted Relaters can often be found leading small group Bible studies, writing blogs, serving on the women's ministry team at church, or at a coffee shop with one or two close friends. You might even find them on the stage as a speaker or on the worship team. Even though they're in a large group, they still feel safe because there's a distance between them and all the people. Because they're introverted, they feel most comfortable in small groups, but they also have an intense desire for relationship with others, and often feel that what they've been through as a person lends itself well to helping others going through the same things. You'll often hear them saying, "I've been through the exact same thing. Let me tell you how God met me there."

Although they tend to develop long-term, committed, deep relationships with others, they can be tempted at times to see this as a weakness, thinking things like, "I'm not enough. I'm not making a big enough difference in people's lives because lots of people overwhelm me. And I'm not fun. Excelling one-on-one and preferring quiet over noise limits what I can do for the Kingdom of God."

As a mom, the Introverted Relater thrives on helping her children understand their own hearts. Communication is her best asset, but she often feels like she's not good enough at having fun or coming up with creative ways to laugh and be spontaneous with her children.

The Introverted Doer

I introduced my friend Jamie to you a few paragraphs above. Jamie is the perfect example of an Introverted Doer. This is how she describes herself: "I treasure the relationships that I have in my life and I long to reach out to others. The easiest way for me to do that is to encourage and help them. It's easier for me to make them dinner, watch their children, or surprise them with chocolate than opening up my heart."

Just like Jamie described, Introverted Doers can often be found serving behind the scenes. They're on the meals ministry at church and always seem to know when a family could use a little boost. They'll show up randomly to clean your house after your baby is born or take your kids for several hours to give you a break after your husband has ACL surgery (yes, Jamie did that for us). Again, as introverts, these people will feel most comfortable in small groups, but unlike the Introverted Relaters, Introverted Doers would rather serve you than talk about the deep things of their lives. In fact, things generally have to be pretty bad for them to open up about their real heart struggles, even to those they're closest to in life. They're happiest when their routine stays intact, and you'll often hear them saying, "What can I do to make things better for you? I'm headed out that way anyway…Why don't I just bring over a meal to make things easier?"

Although they always seem to be there when you need them most, they don't necessarily see this as a strength, thinking things like, "No one sees me because I always serve behind the scenes. I'm not making a big enough difference in people's lives because I struggle to 'be real' with those around me. Excelling in service limits what I can do for the Kingdom of God."

As a mom, the Introverted Doer excels at keeping a schedule and getting things done. She's organized, clean, and always on time, but often struggles to know what to say to really reach the hearts of her kids, and would love to be able to laugh with them more frequently instead of accomplishing everything on her to-do list.

The Extroverted Relater

My friend Erin, who also happens to be the cofounder of the MOB Society, is a classic Extroverted Relater. This is how she describes herself: "My heart yearns to connect with others, making them feel loved and heard through conversation. I come away from coffee dates or even phone calls with friends filled to the brim, even if I have just been listening to them pour out their heart the whole time! However, this love for connecting often causes me to feel stretched thin across all areas of my life."

Like the Introverted Relater, the Extroverted Relater thrives on relationship with others. But unlike the Introverted Relaters, their motto is "the more the merrier." Probably best termed "the life of the party," these people stand out in a crowd. They have lots of friends, and just seem to know a lot of people. They're good networkers, and always seem to know whom to call for help in an emergency. You'll find them serving in ways that connect other people, taking various leadership roles within the church, and loving on as many people as they possibly can. You'll often hear them saying, "I'm so glad to see you! You look beautiful today! Have I introduced you to my friend so and so? You two should really know each other. Excuse me, there's my other friend, gotta run!"

Although their big, funny, warm personalities make them a crowd favorite, Extroverted Relaters don't always see this as a strength, thinking things like, "I'm too much, too loud, and I don't have a gentle and quiet spirit. Others see me as too bubbly and often don't take me seriously. Knowing so many people spreads me too thin and limits what I can do for the Kingdom of God."

The Extroverted Relater is the mom all the other kids wish was theirs. Her house is the fun house, and they don't have to be afraid to be loud. She's great at having fun and making her kids laugh, but sometimes struggles with wanting her kids to really like her, and not just want things from her. Sometimes, she feels defeated when the kids don't take her efforts to connect seriously.

The Extroverted Doer

My friend Logan is the host of Allume, the largest Christian blogging conference in the United States. She is a classic Extroverted Doer. She says about herself, "I love talking to people, but I'm all the time seeing things that need to be done. Someone has to do them, so I just do. However, sometimes my need to do makes it hard to relate to those around me at the level I'd like. At a recent Allume conference, I honestly just needed to go to the bathroom. I *so* didn't want anyone to feel like I didn't want to visit with them so I pretended to talk on my cell phone just to get to the bathroom. It's that bad…I love people so much but I can't pull myself away because there's so much to get done."

Like the Extroverted Relater, she has that classic "larger-than-life" personality, but unlike the Extroverted Relater, she can still get overwhelmed by large groups of people who want to take from her emotional bank. You can usually count on her to say *yes* when you have a need because she knows how to get things done (or knows who to ask if she doesn't). She might be the one heading up, organizing, and planning the women's event of the year, and you'll find her with a totally overwhelmed schedule—going, going, going—until she's completely exhausted—but loving every second of it. You'll often hear her saying, "I'd be happy to run that committee. Yes, I can organize the bake sale. Sure! I'd be happy to be in charge of planning the prayer and praise night!"

She comes across as a very capable person, and likely is, but Extroverted Doers don't always see their abilities as a strength, thinking things like, "I have a hard time getting to the heart level with people, and this limits what I can do for the Kingdom of God."

As a mom, the Extroverted Doer is the ultimate fun mom. She crafts, she inspires, she organizes, she makes memories—all on the fly. But sometimes she feels defeated because she doesn't know how to reach her children's hearts when it seems to matter most.

Get Yourself Filled

Do you see what I'm getting at, ladies? Each of the women I described above has obvious gifts. God created each of them to uniquely contribute something to his work here on earth, both as a mom and a woman. But we're so busy dwelling on what we're not that we forget what we've got.

Today, I want to encourage you to live freely in who God made you to be. Let me share a brief story to explain what I mean.

As you might imagine, Valentine's Day is my least favorite holiday. Not because I don't love to make the people in my life feel special, but because what used to be a simple holiday where kids shared cheap cards with their friends has become Pinterest-ified. And by that, I mean that moms are now heading to Pinterest to seek out the means and instructions to create magazine-worthy Valentines. Gone are the days when kids could just share a simple note telling a friend they were special. Now they have to give away special pencils or cut out bears with hearts or bake homemade cookies. Sometimes it even involves a glue gun—shock! Gasp! You get the picture.

I just don't have it in me to participate in the Pinterest race. I'm not saying it's all bad. Certainly if crafting is your gift, you should use it to bless your family and the other special people in your life. But every year I walk away from Valentine's Day feeling like I've let my kids down because we still buy the good, old-fashioned box of cards. And that's all.

I think sometimes we're tempted to look at Pinterest and think the screenshot of crafts and devotions and "six steps to spice up your marriage when you co-sleep with your kids" in front of us all came from one mom. Not true. There are literally millions of moms creating for Pinterest that make it the powerhouse it is.

Friend, the same thing is true of your life…and mine.

This year, as I stood at our homeschool party and watched the kids exchange gifts, it dawned on me. My boys may not have a mom who has the ability to patiently teach them how to create a spectacular Valentine's Day gift. They may not have a mom who can put together an amazing Science party for them. And they may not have a mom who will ever love noise and large groups of people. But they *do* have a mom who can explain life to them in biblical terms. They *do* have a mom who can teach them the value of honest, good communication, and they *do* have a mom who can teach them how to have solid, biblical relationships.

Even better? In our little group of friends, the people we do community with on a daily basis, there's a crafty mom, a servant mom, a musical mom, and a teacher mom. All of the areas that best define my weaknesses are represented in this group. That makes us a powerhouse.

I could look at these women, each of whom is gifted at something totally different from me, and wish I could be more like them. I could spend my days wishing I could do a great job at reaching the hearts of my boys and be the fun mom. Or I could spend my days being thankful that God has surrounded me with friends who bring variety to my life. They fill my gaps, and that's an amazing gift from

God. Why? Because we weren't meant to do life alone. God created us for community—created us to need each other to do life well. He created you that way too.

We weren't created to be good at everything, but we're great at some things. So let's vow to let God use us effectively in those areas, and fill the gaps with His grace and good friends.

Don't complicate your life by wishing you were someone else. Be good at who you are—who God made you to be. Know who God says you are, and trust Him to fill in the gaps.

Let go of what you're not, and hold on to what you've got.

◇◇◇

In 1 Corinthians 12:14, 17-18 we find these words:

> "For the body does not consist of one member
> but of many…if the whole body were an eye,
> where would be the sense of hearing? If the whole body
> were an ear, where would be the sense of smell? But as
> it is,
> God has arranged the members of the body,
> each one of them, as he chose."

Just for fun, imagine the verses above read more like this:

> "For the mamas do not consist of one type but of many
> amazingly different kinds. If every mama was crafty,
> who would organize? If every mama was the life of the
> party, who would bring meals to the sick? But as it is,
> God has arranged the mamas, each one of them,
> as he chose. And they are beautiful, and reflect His grace,
> when they know it, and walk out life together."

◇◇◇

Chapter 3

Confronting Carol

Stacey

The dishes in my sink could have their own zip code. There has been a fort in my living room for days. My daughter has pirated all my best decorations to decorate said fort. The baby is wrapped around my leg eating something she may have found on the floor. I'm searching for something under the couch when it hits me, "Where do I start?"

I had no idea what I wanted to be when I grew up. It wasn't that I didn't have hopes and dreams. I suppose I did. Living in a small town, I was happy, content, and safe. My dreams involved being a professional cheerleader or singing on Broadway. At some point, these dreams just seemed a little bit ridiculous, so I focused on getting good grades and attending a good school.

The truth is, I always knew I would be a mom. I loved playing dolls as a girl living at 29 Lincoln Avenue. In fact, I probably played with dolls much longer than other girls. I remember the last doll I received for Christmas. She wore a cream colored dress and had blue eyes that blinked shut when I lay her down to sleep. There was a struggle in my heart that year to grow up, and a fight to stay young. Luckily for me, this also coincided somewhat with my babysitting years. I could now dress and keep real babies who smelled like baby powder and apple juice. In the years that followed, while other more popular girls went on dates, I spent Saturday nights putting other peoples' babies to bed and watching MTV. I dreamed about being a good mom and the home I would one day keep.

Fifteen years ago I sat in a wheelchair as a nurse in pink scrubs wheeled me to the curb, amazed by the brand new baby girl in my arms. While my husband pulled around with the car, I remember thinking, *Do they know I'm leaving here with her? Do they really think I have what it takes to be a good mom?*

I guess I always knew how to be a good mom. My version was somewhere between Carol Brady and Caroline Ingalls. For the sake of consistency, we should call this good mom Carol. Carol woke up every morning with a smile on her face. She whipped up a magnificent healthy breakfast for her growing brood while her whites were soaking in Clorox in the washing machine. She sparkled with grace and quite frankly her favorite part of day was when the kids would come downstairs for breakfast. She clearly had a good handle on this mommy thing.

The best part about Carol was that she always had time for her kids. She and her kids had lots of wisdom-filled conversations while eating homemade chocolate chip cookies after school. Her kids would say, "Wow, Mom, you are the best." She knew it was true.

At night, Carol was tired but not exhausted. She slept with her makeup perfectly in place and a smile on her lips. Life as mom was good. She was good. *And she was enough.*

I see her staring at me with her hands on her hips. She judges me. She makes me feel less than. She reminds me that I will never measure up. She sighs a lot, pushing me to keep going when I have nothing left to give. Carol is no longer my graceful and sparkly role model or the mom I believe I can be. She is my phantom. And most days, I just can't seem to get her out of my kitchen or my heart.

I have never felt this more than since the birth of my fourth daughter. Yes, I know the fact that I have four girls sounds adorable. I know right now you may be thinking about *Little Women*, Jo, Marmie, and how sweet four girls sound. Or perhaps you are thinking, *Wow, I have a daughter and she is much tougher to raise than my son.* Maybe you are, in the kindness of your heart, saying a little prayer for me. Bless your heart if you did.

The truth is, being a mom to four girls has been both a wonderful and humbling work for me. It is a dig down deep, throw your hands to the heavens, beg for mercy kind of work that can't be pushed aside. Most days I find myself completely obliterated of wisdom, strength, and humor. I collapse in my bed wondering how in the world I am going to do it again, *tomorrow.*

I am not so good at it. I stumble and fumble all day long with an audience of four watching. For the first time in my life, I am leaning 100 percent into the grace God gives me every day. See, in every other occupation I have had, I was able to perform, perfect, and rise above any expectation applied to the position. This has not been the case, and I suspect never will be, in my mothering.

I suppose, too, no other occupation has meant as much to me as this one does. What is on the line is not a promotion or a slap on the back of praise. It is the very hearts of my kids. And it demands a pouring out and pressing on like I have never experienced before.

I put expectations on myself. I feel expectations from others. I crumble under falling short of the expectations of my children. In the middle of it all, I am broken and weary. I feel the pressure every day that I need to be amazing…and I'm fresh out of amazing.

And what do you do when you're fresh out of amazing? For a while, I pretended like everything was normal. I smiled and put on my MAC under-eye cream and my Smashbox lip gloss and I covered up the broken and weary mom with a veil. *I hid behind fine.*

I was far from fine. I had waves of discouragement. In fact, I swam in it. I wondered how in the world I was going to make it each day. And since I am being honest, I will go ahead and tell you, I had thoughts that scared me. I told no one.

But the day I wrote the original blog post that became the book you now hold in your hands, something happened. I said it out loud.

I raised my little white flag and I said, "I am not amazing. I am not fine." I started writing right where I was. It wasn't pretty. In fact, it was kind of messy. And in the middle of the mess I did not see critical Carol. I saw a loving God who wanted to meet me in the middle of it all.

<hr />

He doesn't need me to be amazing.
Turns out he has that covered already.

<hr />

I remember a short time after writing the first blog post that would become *Hope for the Weary Mom*, a friend stopped me at church. She said, "Wow, you were so honest." I said something like, "Yeah, I guess I was." As I walked away, all I could think of was that the veil was finally off. And I was terrified. *What would others think of me?*

One of my favorite books is *The Pursuit of God*, by A.W. Tozer. In it he says:

> Let us remember that when we talk of the rending of the veil we are speaking in a figure, and the thought of it is poetical, almost pleasant, but in actuality, there is nothing pleasant about it. In human experience that veil is made of living spiritual tissue; it is composed of sentient, quivering stuff of which our whole beings consist, and to touch it is to touch us where we feel pain. To tear it away is to injure us, to hurt us and make us bleed...it is never fun to die.[1]

It has taken me forty years and four babies to finally get to this place of removing the veil of "fine." It has not been fun. In particular, the last four years have not been easy. But they have been necessary. See, I've been learning that I am not the good mom I always wanted to be. I don't have it all together. I am instead, a dependent mom who is learning to live honestly where she is. I am a veil-torn mom who sees that in order to come face to face with grace, I had to be brought low and to the end of myself. I am a weary mom who is reaching out for hope and holding on with both hands.

I close my eyes and finally ask for help. "Jesus, come today. Come here today. In my mess. To my kitchen, but first to my heart. I am in need of your grace." It is funny how, as soon as I call for Hope, he comes running and brings his Word to wrap around my heart.

⬦⬦⬦⬦⬦⬦⬦⬦⬦⬦⬦⬦⬦⬦⬦⬦⬦⬦⬦⬦⬦⬦⬦⬦⬦⬦⬦⬦⬦⬦⬦⬦

Hope is not a wish or a sprinkle of magical fairy dust.
Hope is a person.

⬦⬦⬦⬦⬦⬦⬦⬦⬦⬦⬦⬦⬦⬦⬦⬦⬦⬦⬦⬦⬦⬦⬦⬦⬦⬦⬦⬦⬦⬦⬦⬦

Hope is not a wish or a sprinkle of magical fairy dust. Hope is a person. Hope comes with flesh and blood in Jesus. When I call to him, he comes quickly. He has no expectations of me. Actually, it is quite the opposite. He says things like:

> Do not fear, for I am with you;
> Do not anxiously look about you, for I am your God.
> I will strengthen you, surely I will help you,
> Surely I will uphold you with My righteous right hand"
> (Isaiah 41:10 NASB).

> "Come to me, all of you who are weary and carry heavy burdens, and I will give you rest" (Matthew 11:28 NLT).

He wants to help me. He wants to comfort me. He wants to lift my heavy burdens and give me sweet soul rest. When I am honest about my struggle and I take off the veil, I am in place to receive this comfort. There is nothing between us, and hope reaches straight to my heart.

As I open my eyes, I see the dishes are still close to a national disaster. Nothing has really changed in a physical sense. I get up, and the tears start to flow a bit. He leans in close and whispers it again, "Surely I will help you. Surely."

And he does.

When Others Are Drawn Into Your Story

Friendship…is born at the moment
when one man says to another, "What! You too?
I thought that no one but myself…"
—C.S. Lewis[2]

Another thing happened when I raised my little white flag from the messy depths of my heart. I found out that to my surprise, I was not the only mom who felt this way. Time and time again other moms have said, "What! You too?" As much as I wanted to run back into hiding when my friend stopped me at church, I realized that by saying it out loud, I may have sounded a trumpet call for other moms who felt the same way to join me in the journey from weariness to hope. Was it possible that in telling my story, other moms might see themselves too? Did they have their own version of Carol lurking in the shadows of their hearts?

Author Emily P. Freeman said in her book *Grace for the Good Girl,* "I believe women need to talk about the ways we hide, the longing to be known, the fear in the knowing. Beyond that, I believe in the life-giving power of story, in the beauty of vulnerability and in the strength that is found in weakness."[3]

My fear has always been tied to the illusion that other moms have it all together and I don't. I have hidden for years because I was afraid that they would not understand my broken places. As it turns out, I was hiding from women who felt just like me. They were not judging me. They were simply busy hiding in their messy kitchens, probably thinking I was judging them, too. Truthfully, what we really needed was an invitation to be drawn into one another's stories and the chance to say, "We are more alike than we know. I know your story. I'm living it too."

The Art of Clumping

Do you know the game Clump? It is like hide and go seek, except one person is doing the hiding and everyone else is searching. When a seeker finds the one hiding she joins her. In the end, you are all together in one big clump, laughing together. I like to think of *Hope for the Weary Mom* as just that. We are all hiding in the middle of our own messes. Wouldn't it be more fun if we were in it together? What if instead of hiding alone we clumped?

The truth is, what we really need is Jesus. But he knows, more than we do, that we were made to live in community. He has always been a fan of the buddy system. After all, didn't Adam have Eve? Naomi had Ruth, and David had Jonathan. God never planned on us living a hope-filled life alone. His design was that we would walk with others for a lifetime.

But sometimes life gets busy with diapers and chores and getting through the day and we forget what we were made for. We forget our design. We don't even realize we miss it until one day we are alone and desperate for just one person to know our hearts. What do we do when we are ready to clump and find a few friends to tell our stories to and find encouragement for our most weary days?

Ask God to bring a friend into your life.
Ask him to build your own clump.

Ask God to bring a friend into your life. Ask him to build your own clump.

We don't know how or when God will bring this about for you. But we are believing with you that God will begin to build a community of other moms in your life. Why? We have seen him do that in our own lives. We've lived weary and alone, and we've seen the fruit that comes from trusting God and sharing our lives with others who understand. God has a plan, and he does not work on our timetable. Building deep community takes time. But the good news is, you can start now. You may have to be brave and step out of your comfort zone. When we moved to a new town, I had to put on my brave shoes many times and initiate conversations with strangers. Some of those friendships did not last. Some stuck and are still with me today.

Don't Bump or Dump When You Clump

Building community always brings a risk factor because other people are human just like us. We didn't say community was perfect. Sometimes we run into moms who bump or dump.

The Bumper. She is the queen of comparison. She says things like, "My kids are better, smarter than your kids. Have you seen my new purse from the clearance rack at TJ Maxx? Designer and 99 percent off. By the way, my husband is taking me to a fancy dinner and a movie. He really loves me." This mom is trying to feel better by elevating herself over other moms.

The Dumper. She is the downer of the group. She says things like, "My life is ruined. My laundry is never done. I have no hope. Can you fix me?" This mom is trying to feel better by gaining your sympathy.

What about you? Have you ever been the *Bumper* or the *Dumper* in your group of friends? I'm sure we all have at one point or another. When you see other moms engaging in this type of behavior, give them grace. Our day will come soon enough. We need grace from them just like they need it from us. In the meantime, remember these three things:

1. Continue to let God mold and make you into the woman he wants you to be. Don't wait. Walk with him now. It is true, you have to be the friend others want to have in order to get a friend you want to keep.

2. Strive to be a healthy clumper yourself. Don't bump or dump when you clump.

3. Friends don't complete us. Friends complement us. Only God can fill your heart with hope. True friends will point you to him.

In the Meantime

Sometimes it takes a while for the truth to sink in. When we're weary, hurt, and disappointed with life it can be good to open our hearts to others and walk through the valley willingly together. We know it can be scary to think of opening up those dark places, but there's really nothing to be afraid of when you embrace the truths we've set before you here. At other times, we are called to a foreign land. We are alone and we don't know a soul there. What do we do on those days?

A few years ago, I found myself in exactly that same situation. I have always been a girl who loves connecting with other women. I have joined Bible studies and led small groups numerous times. My heart loves nothing more than meeting friends for coffee and catching a chick flick. But suddenly I was in a new town with a three-year-old and a baby. My husband had a new job working long hours and I was alone much of the day. I remember after my daughter was born, shortly before Christmas, the nurse said to me, "Isn't anyone going to come and see you?" Obviously hormonal, I held back tears and said, "We just moved here. I don't know anyone." I think that made her feel worse than I did at the time. She made a point to come visit me while I was recovering.

After bringing home my bundle of Christmas Grace, no one brought food. We had no visitors. We eagerly awaited the arrival of family who would come after the holidays to help us settle in our new home and with our newest addition. Their visit seemed all too short and once again I faced long days and nights feeling disconnected.

I did what I knew to do. I cried out to the Lord. I had a really long talk with him one evening on my way to the grocery store. I told him I was tired and lonely. What I really needed, I reminded him, was someone to say my name. Does that sound silly to you? Well, remember, I grew up in a small town. The old saying "Everybody knows everybody" is true. I went to a college where I had a few good friends already. I roomed with lifelong friends who knew me. This was the first time in my life I did not really know anyone. And no one, I mean no one, knew my name. So this mattered a great deal to me.

I grabbed my cart and tried to remember what we needed in our pantry at home. I was every kind of weary and worn. I looked it, too. My hair was a mess and I'm not sure I had bothered doing my makeup that day. I noticed the two girls almost immediately when I started down the aisle. They were having way too much fun for me. Clearly, they were friends enjoying an inside joke. I found myself annoyed and jealous at the same time. I passed by them quickly, reaching for a jar of spaghetti sauce. When I got to the end of the aisle, one of the girls said, "She wants to know if your name is Stacey." I stopped suddenly in my tracks. "Did she just say my name? MY NAME?" I looked back at the girls, searching their faces for familiarity. "Yes," I said, "that is my NAME."

As it turns out, the girl who knew me was an old friend from college. I did not recognize her because she had dyed her hair blonde. She was living and working in town for a short time. We chatted and exchanged numbers. She left and I went back to shopping. As I made my way to the parking lot I was overcome with tears once again. God was the one who spoke my name that day. I have treasured the sound deep within my heart ever since. Known and noticed, my identity was found in who he was, not where I lived. He had not lost sight of me or forgotten where I was either.

Over the period of the next couple of years, God began to build community in my life. I found a sweet group of sisters to share life with on a daily basis. We clumped in the best way possible—around a table studying God's Word. Our hearts and stories connected deeply. They showed up in droves when our third daughter arrived—and with enough food to feed an army. The contrast was amazing. I smiled at the way God had provided. I also enjoyed being spoiled.

Still, I will not discount the lonely years. They served a purpose in my life. I walked closely with Jesus because I did not have anyone other than my husband and my girls to cling to. I look at those days as a time where God was doing a specific work. I am grateful now for those days. But I can also see how he was working behind the scenes and preparing me for a new, richer community of women who became sisters of my heart.

Where are you today, friend? Are you trying desperately to measure up to the perfect mom who lives in your head or heart? I was. Are you longing for a community of your own but scared to death to share your story and open your heart? I've been there, too. Nothing keeps us weary like the illusion that everyone else has it all together. What if we looked up instead of sizing up? What if, after we found our hope in him, we shared our own life-giving story? I think other moms would come running with stories of their own. Together we would all get to point to him. He'd get the glory. Hope would spread.

I'm game. Are you?

Chapter 4

The Marathon of Mothering

Stacey

$\mathcal{I}$'ve heard a lot of talk lately about the seasons of motherhood and how it gets easier. There is a part of my heart wanting this to be true. But now, fifteen years into my own mothering journey, I'm starting to believe this is more wishful thinking than Gospel truth.

I remember one of my first indications that mothering would require complete devotion, and that my course was mapped out a bit differently than I imagined. My husband and I were in Colorado for the biannual national staff conference for Campus Crusade for Christ. At this time, we were a family of four. I decided to place our oldest, who was almost four, in childcare during the conference so I could attend a few of the meetings. Our youngest was only a few months old so I kept her with me. A couple of days into the conference our oldest picked up a flu bug and was sick. This is a pretty normal moment in the life of a mother, right? Sick kids go with the territory. But this typical mommy moment was highlighted with another event that marked our ministry tremendously.

Our founder and president, Bill Bright, had been ill for some time and passed away while our staff of 6,000 gathered for one of our evening sessions. However, our family was not at the meeting. We were back at our apartment with our sick child. Someone knocked on our door to tell us the news and to alert my husband,

Mike. He was part of a technology team who had created a website to be used in the event of Dr. Bright's passing. It needed to go live immediately. He was the guy to do it. He grabbed his computer and flew out the door. As it swung shut my daughter ran to the bathroom. My youngest was crying in her Pack 'n Play and I stood speechless. As news of Dr. Bright's homegoing spread quickly, our staff family, having left the evening meeting, flooded back into the gymnasium at Colorado State University. Gratitude for the life of one so faithful prompted spontaneous worship to the Lord. It was a holy, defining moment in the life of our ministry. God was so gracious to us that we were all together at this time.

It was also a defining moment for me. I wanted desperately to be swept up in that corporate moment as well. But my place was with my girls who needed my physical presence, prayers, and mercy more than anything. Weariness settled a bit that day as I comforted both of my girls and wondered why mothering felt like such a lonely event at times.

That same four-year-old is now a teenager. The physical weariness I felt during her toddler years has faded and been replaced with an emotional weariness I feel almost daily. We are making decisions this week that will most likely affect the rest of her life. I am encouraging her and training her on a completely different level these days. Someone once told me, "Little kids, little problems. Big kids, bigger problems." I wouldn't exactly say she has big problems, but her problems seem bigger than they did when she was smaller. If *these* are the easy days I have been promised, I want to understand what the definition of *easy* truly is. Oh, I think they mean well by trying to hold the light up at the end of a long tunnel. More and more I'm seeing motherhood as a marathon of endurance, not a sprint to the next stage of life. There is no other calling in life that mixes the possibility for body and soul weariness with triumph and trials. It shifts. It changes almost daily. But does it get easier?

- Is it easier to hold a colicky baby or a teen who has made a bad choice?

- Is it easier to never leave the house because of sick kids or to watch your kids leave the house for college?

- Is it easier to worry they'll never make friends or worry about the friends they've made?

We are moms. We are called to love well and be faithful. And there is nothing easy about doing these two things for what adds up to a lifetime. This commitment alone can cause weariness to settle deep within our hearts. In the marathon of motherhood they hand you a person, not a baton. And you don't cross a magical finish line when they graduate from high school. You run it for life—yours and theirs—and the thing Jesus will hopefully say to you when you see him face to face is, "You ran well, mom. You ran well."

But how we do we run well in the marathon of mothering? How do we map out a course that will condition our hearts for the long road home? Because really, this is what motherhood is all about.

A Short Walk That Took 40 Years

I have a deep love of Scripture. I find it amazing that God has been so completely honest with us in how his people have walked with him (or not) throughout the ages. Many of the stories he could have chosen to leave out because, let's face it, they are pretty gritty. But God, in his infinite wisdom, knew we would need these examples of humanity for our own stories to be written with grace. He knew we'd need to see people just like us fail and then find redemption and rescue in him.

When I think of long roads home, I think of the nation of Israel. They turned a short

> Motherhood is not only about raising little people to become thriving, Jesus-loving adults. Motherhood is also about him making me into his faithful daughter.

walk into a lifetime journey. This was, to be sure, partly due to the fact that they had a knack for making bad choices. Yet in the process, God turned them into a people he called his own. I think their story, more than any other, reminds me that motherhood is not only about raising little people to become thriving, Jesus-loving adults. Motherhood is also about him making me into his faithful daughter. While I'm busy checking off milestones for my children, God is checking off mine, too.

> There is none like you, O LORD, and there is no God besides you, according to all that we have heard with our ears. And who is like your people Israel, the one nation on earth whom God went to redeem to be his people, making for yourself a name for great and awesome things, in driving out nations before your people whom you redeemed from Egypt? And you made your people Israel to be your people forever, and you, O LORD, became their God (1 Chronicles 17:20-22).

So how did God redeem his people? He rescued them from a tyrant king in Egypt who had been bossing them around for hundreds of years. He did great and mighty acts. He led them, he fed them, and in the end he turned their hearts toward his. The story is undeniably written Hollywood style. It is epic, as my daughter would say.

I love the reminder from Hebrews 13:8 that "Jesus Christ is the same, yesterday, today, and forever." This same God writes my story as well. It is also epic—at least for the people in my home and in my heart. I think aspects of Israel's journey can provide a powerful parallel throughout my own personal marathon of mothering.

There Is a Plan

God's plan does not always make sense at the time. God promised to take Israel to the Promised Land. The route he chose was not the shortest or the easiest. But God had a reason for leading them where and how he chose. He was teaching them to be faithful, to depend on him.

My friend Krystal is a real runner. She once told me about a marathon she ran at Disney World. Near the end of the course they had to run uphill and around a curve and the finish line was nowhere in sight. She wanted to quit. But just when she was plotting her own demise she spotted the finish line. It was behind the scenes somewhere near the Epcot parking lot. Did it make sense at the time? No. But Mickey and Minnie Mouse were there with cold water and a medal to place around her neck. The part of the race where Krystal wanted to quit is where her marathon was won. She dug deep. She trusted something bigger than herself. And she kept running.

God's plan for my mothering does not always make sense to me either. How do I parent a child who is just like me? Or what about the one who is nothing like me? When I pour out my life day in and day out and they don't notice how much I do for them, how is this better than hearing them say, "Thank you?" I don't know. But here is what I do know. This place—and sometimes it feels like a desert— is where God is teaching me to depend on him. I am learning to be faithful where I am. I'm learning to call out to him. I'm learning to dig deep into grace and allow him to be all I need.

There Is a Pace

God was not worried about getting Israel from point A to point B in record time. They spent their long years walking and waiting. Was God slow in keeping his promise? It might have seemed that way. God's presence set the pace for their journey.

> And the LORD went before them by day in a pillar of cloud to lead them along the way, and by night in a pillar of fire to give them light, that they might travel by day and by night. The pillar of cloud by day and the pillar of fire by night did not depart from before the people (Exodus 13:21-22).

He led with a cloud by day and a pillar of fire at night. If the cloud moved, the people moved. When the pillar of fire stopped, the people stopped. Sometimes they camped in one location for weeks. Other times they journeyed on and on for days. I can imagine them watching daily and saying, "Did God move? Is he still with us? Where is he going? Will today be the day?" The anticipation must have been great. I'm sure the waiting was also difficult to bear at times.

Runners tell me the most important part of a long run has to do with the pace they run. If you start out too fast you will wear yourself out too quickly and have nothing left at the end. Their pace is directly influenced by where they fix their eyes. As it turns out, when you look in the wrong place it affects your entire body and how fast you run. I found this fascinating:

> Focusing your gaze on points that are in close proximity to your current position will result in greater stress and mental fatigue...When focusing or "fixating" on a point much further away, you will find that you will run more easily and freely, and feel as though you are being pulled toward that point.[1]

Some days as a mom I am tempted to look at my right now mess and wish for a different day. The points closest to me cause me stress and weariness. If I want to run freely and be pulled along the journey, guess where I need to look?

> Therefore, since we are surrounded by so great a cloud of witnesses, let us also lay aside every weight, and sin which clings so closely, and let us run with endurance the race that is set before us, looking to Jesus, the founder and perfecter of our faith, who for the joy that was set before him endured the cross, despising the shame, and is seated at the right hand of the throne of God.

Consider him who endured from sinners such hostility against himself, so that you may not grow weary or faint-hearted (Hebrews 12:1-3).

We look to Jesus. He is our cloud by day and our pillar of fire by night. He has gone before us, and as we set our gaze on him we are pulled toward him and our eternal home. I see him standing beyond the finish line. He is there, and this is where my weary eyes need to be locked every day so I too can keep the steady pace of this mothering race.

There Is a Provision

When they were slaves in Egypt, Israel had a place to sleep and food on their tables. Undeniably, it was also oppressive and grueling. But sometimes even in our most difficult places we have a small bit of control. They knew how to find food. They knew how to survive.

But what kind of food does one find in the desert? What do you eat when all you can see for miles is sand? The livestock was running out and what they carried with them out of Egypt had not lasted long. And so they did what many of us do in similar situations. They complained.

> *As soon as* they got to the desert *of Sin,* the entire community of Israelites complained to Moses and Aaron. **Israelites:** It would have been better if we had died by the hand of the Eternal in Egypt. At least *we had plenty to eat and drink, for* our pots were stuffed with meat and we had as much bread as we wanted. But now you have brought the entire community out to the desert to starve us to death (Exodus 16:2-3 THE VOICE).

This sounds like my house every day around 5:30 p.m. I'm sure you've heard something similar at your house, too. But God did not bring them to the desert to starve them to death.

Eternal One *(to Moses)*: *Rest assured,* I have heard the *constant* complaining of the Israelites. Tell them, "In the evening, you will have meat to eat; and in the morning, you will have enough bread to satisfy your *gnawing* hunger. Then you will know that I am the Eternal your God (Exodus 16:12 THE VOICE).

I think He allowed them to feel real hunger so he could feed them and be their provision. He wanted to be their source. Daily they gathered bread and meat and were fed by their God.

Don't we do the same thing, friend? We are hungry and so we complain. But we need him to fill our hearts, not our stomachs. We say things like, "I'm here and I'm dying, Lord. I can't take another step in this journey as a mom. Where is my bread?"

I am the bread of life (John 6:48).

There is no doubt that he is the soul food we need in the middle of our weariness. Just like the Israelites gathered enough manna for each day, we too need to gather from God's Word daily. He wants to be our source as well. We have this promise to remind us: "For whatever was written in former days was written for our instruction, that through endurance and through the encouragement of the Scriptures we might have hope" (Romans 15:4).

Let's go back to the race analogy one more time. Here we are, running, running, running, and Jesus offers us fuel to keep us going. Only it isn't water or a power bar. He is holding out hope to us and it is in the form of his Word. Do we keep running and say, "Oh, no thanks, Jesus, I'm good. I don't need any hope today." Or do we receive it, let it encourage us, and find strength to keep going? Great runners do not refuse nourishment they know will get them to the finish line. How can we be any different?

The marathon of mothering certainly takes mental toughness and dedication to keep going. We have a plan marked out and his presence in our lives to show us the way. God sees the beginning and the end in one glance. We can run on, trusting he will provide what we need especially in the most wearying of days.

> I look behind me and you're there, then up ahead and you're there, too—your reassuring presence, coming and going" (Psalm 139:5 MSG).

Jesus is with us every step of the way. He is coaching us, encouraging us to keep going. He runs beside us and helps us carry the load. The beauty of it all is we do not run alone. No matter how much we want to quit. Yes, even on those days.

Camping Out

Sometimes as moms we want nothing more than to do the opposite of running. We want to cease from all forward movement and spend an enormous amount of time idle. Our uniform for the opposite of running is yoga pants and a hoodie. Which when you think of it looks a lot like something you would wear while running. This does not faze us one bit. We want to take lounging to a new level and have enough snacks and entertainment nearby so we can enjoy our vegetation without having to exert much (if any) effort. Personally, my snack of choice would include any, if not all, of the following: sea salt popcorn, M&M's, Java Chip Starbucks Ice Cream in a personalized pint, and Twizzlers. Well, I might have to forgo the Twizzlers these days. But I would want them. Entertainment is easy, because *Downton Abbey* is now on *Netflix*. We could camp out here for a good week and not break a sweat or lift a finger. It sounds good on so many levels.

Israel camped too. For one thing, God told them to camp. He led them there. But I happen to think they were finished with running and escaping and carrying every bit of their lives on their backs, too. They were weary in every way. They certainly had come to a place where the plan was not making much sense. For heaven's sake, there was a large body of water in front of them and no boat was going to hold close to a million family members. They were tired and they were afraid. Yes, camping made the most sense.

Meanwhile, who came running at full speed hot on their trail? Their greatest enemy:

> "The Egyptians pursued them, all Pharaoh's horses and chariots and his horsemen and his army, and overtook them encamped at the sea" (Exodus 14:9).

This will probably not come as a shock to you, but guess what Israel did? They complained and asked Moses, their leader, why he didn't just let them die in Egypt, back where they were slaves. Moses tried to reassure them and then he gave them God's message:

> "Why do you call for Me? Instruct the Israelites to *break camp and* keep moving. Raise your staff and reach out over the sea to divide it" (Exodus 14:15-16 THE VOICE).

Can you imagine what the people thought when Moses said, "Get up. Break Camp. God is going to make a way out of here. THROUGH the sea." I'm guessing many of them thought he was crazy. Some might have thought in the middle of their fearful place this would be a fine place to just dig a grave. But God had another word for them:

> The LORD will fight for you, and you have only to be silent (Exodus 14:14).

Israel watched as God not only parted the sea in front of them but moved the cloud of his presence, which had always been in front of them, and placed it between them and the Egyptians.

He went before them.

He went behind them.

He fought for them.

Hope made a way when there was none to be found.

Thus the LORD saved Israel that day from the hand of the Egyptians, and Israel saw the Egyptians dead on the seashore. Israel saw the great power that the LORD used against the Egyptians, so the people feared the LORD, and they believed in the LORD and in his servant Moses" (Exodus 14:30-31).

Remember I told you it was epic? God told Israel to break camp and move forward before the Red Sea parted, before his presence had moved behind them. He had spoken his word. They were to move before they saw him fulfill his promise to fight.

So this is the place in the story where it gets personal. I understand what staying back at camp looks like. I see myself with fear and trembling, looking around saying, "You want me to do what?" I was here in this all too familiar place a few days ago. Only the Red Sea God needed to part was more like writing a book in the nooks and crannies of my life while trying to be a wife and mother of four. Does that not sound like a miracle to you? I assure you it is. And the enemy barking at me from behind was a health concern. I sat down by the fire and cried. I also grabbed my dark chocolate M&M's and said, "This place right here is going to be a fine place to dig a grave. Pass the ice cream, please. I'm done."

And then God spoke through my sweet friend Brooke the words of Exodus 14:14. I was reminded that even when weariness and fear say no, hope says go. The road home is long, but you are not alone. *I will fight for you.*

The truth is, life as a mother doesn't get easier because we have an enduring call on our lives. Mother Teresa once said, "We do nothing. God does everything. All glory must return to him. God has not called me to be successful. He called me to be faithful." As he matures our children, he is molding our hearts as well. He is making us mamas more like his Son. The more he chips away what doesn't look like him in my life, the closer he gets to the places that hurt most deeply. I think I'm seeing glimpses of who I'm becoming while at the same time releasing my girls into his hands. There are rewards on both accounts. More and more, I'm fixing my gaze on him. I can see him standing just across the finish line. He is smiling. And I'm going to keep running.

Chapter 5

Redeeming Mommy Guilt

Stacey

I sat across the table from her with a notebook and pen quietly in front of me. My black paperback *NIV Student Bible* was placed neatly beside my notebook. I was ready to absorb every bit of wisdom she had because quite frankly, I was pretty sure mine had all run out. "Stacey, I think the thing that may hinder you most is your desire to please people. In fact, I think if you don't work on this now, it will follow you around for the rest of your life," she said gently but firmly.

At this point, all I wanted to do was please her. So when she handed me the book *Search for Significance,* by Robert S. McGee, I promised to take it back to my room and complete every personality test the book suggested. Days later we met at the same table in the same corner of the dining hall. I think she smartly brought me a loaf of her famous poppy seed bread to sweeten the discussion a bit.

"Fear of failure dominates your life," she read. "If you don't do something about it now, it will not go away on its own."

"Wow. That is pretty brutal," I remarked. "Does it really say *dominates your life?*"

Yes. It did. In fact, every test I took from this smart little book pretty much said the same exact thing.

Feelings of shame dominate your life.
The fear of punishment dominates your life.
The fear of rejection dominates your life.

At least I was consistent in my scores, you might say. I had always been a good test taker. Or in this case, was I a bad test taker? What I remember from this mentoring moment with someone I greatly respected was for the first time in my life, my cover was blown. *I was afraid of failing. I was highly motivated by what others thought of me. I had a hard time saying no when asked to do anything for anyone. I wanted people to like me.* Was that so bad? Apparently, it was because it dominated my life.

I squirmed in my seat and took a bite of bread. *What do I do now?*

My mentor was wise enough to put her arm around me and give me encouragement that day. She handed me the book, gave me a few pages to read, and reminded me there was hope for girls like me. She knew, because she was more like me than I knew.

I took the book and placed it in my backpack when I returned to Indiana University in the fall of 1991. Sometime after that day, I sat with my roommate Robin and gave her the same tests from the book. I remember adding up her scores and discovering we were both on the same search for more grace in our lives. She scored as brilliantly as I had. We found this hysterical at the time. We were pretty messed up but at least we had each other. And that somehow made it easier to move forward.

I didn't know it then, but grace was on the move in my life and looking for more space to rest and refresh my people-pleasing heart. Guilt gave it a good fight, but in those days I had hours to pour over the truth from my Student Bible. Grace continued to woo me through the Word and eventually won out. I took Ephesians 2:8-9 to heart: "For by grace you have been saved through faith. And this is not of your own doing; it is a gift of God, not a result of works, so that no one may boast." I finally believed this to be true: Grace means I am working *from* acceptance, not *toward* it.

I was 22 when I graduated from Indiana University and a few months later I married the best guy I knew. I met Mike the summer grace showed up in my life in Ocean City. We worked together in the same office, bought a cute little house, and dreamed of starting our family.

> I finally believed this to be true: Grace means I am working *from* acceptance, not *toward* it.

I have come to realize now, some 20 years later, we learn lessons in stages. It is almost like the layers of our heart are peeled back like an onion. We learn one lesson and we think, "Ahh, I've got it." Until one day we don't get it anymore. At this point, God takes his holy hands and peels back another layer. This time, he probes a little deeper. It feels somehow like *déjà vu*. "Haven't I been in the place before?" we might say to ourselves. The truth is we have been here before and yet we haven't. Some lessons are so important we get to learn them more than once.

Lately I've been relearning so many things I thought I understood. There are places in my heart I would have promised you I dealt with years ago. Did I change or shrink back? It was as though I received my bachelors in truth once upon a time, and now I was trying to get my masters in guilt. So God sweetly

> Guilt has no place in a space of grace.

sent me back to the classroom of grace called mothering. I've been learning once again that guilt has no place in a space of grace.

✧✧✧✧✧✧✧✧✧✧✧✧✧✧✧✧✧✧✧✧✧✧✧✧✧✧✧✧✧✧✧

"Great, now I have guilt."
–REX THE DINOSAUR, *TOY STORY*

✧✧✧✧✧✧✧✧✧✧✧✧✧✧✧✧✧✧✧✧✧✧✧✧✧✧✧✧✧✧✧

Start a conversation with other moms about mommy guilt and you will get a lively response. Not long ago, I asked a few of my friends what kind of things they felt mommy guilt for on a daily basis. This is what they said. Feel free to place a check mark next to any of the following that also resonate with you.

Guilt over
not volunteering at their school
worrying about my reputation as a mom
how I feed my kids
worrying too much about heart issues
not worrying enough about heart issues
my anger
our educational choices
not being strict enough
not being a super supportive sports mom
spending my alone "me time" running errands
not going on enough date nights with my husband
missing everyday moments
not having the money to do things my kids want to do
not playing with them
being too tired to take them outside
my own limitations from having a chronic illness

not being the crafty mom
being with them but not present
not spending enough one-on-one time with each child
not being the role model I should for my kids
our messy house
when they watch too much television or play too many electronic games

Can you relate to this list? Maybe you want to add one or two of your own? The thing is, every mom feels guilty about something they either have done or haven't done right. Some things we'll own up to feeling guilty about. Other things we wish we could sweep right under the rug—the one we feel guilty about not keeping clean enough.

One Mom's Story

She purchased one of the top brands of detergents for her family because she cared about value and keeping them clean. When they came out with the brand new pod-type packets to throw in your machine, she picked up a box and sat them by the washer. What happened next racked her with mommy guilt for months.

Her little one mistook the packet of laundry soap for candy and ingested the contents. He spent several days on a ventilator as a result. He recovered but it took months to work through the truckload-sized guilt she heaped on her own shoulders as his mom. *I should have known better. What kind of mother am I? If only I had not gone to work that day.* The list grew on and on.

It was an accident. She admitted to me she is a better and stronger mom now having worked through the mommy guilt from the incident. But an interesting thing happened when she shared the story with her local paper. Another larger news outlet picked up the story and a popular mommy blog linked to it. When a friend told her about the blog post, my friend went to check it out. She then made the mistake of reading the comments left by other moms on the story.

Other moms judged. They pointed their mommy finger at one of their own. Some of them said, "How could she?" and "What was that mother thinking?"

And with each comment her mommy guilt returned with a greater vengeance. Here is what she said to me about this time in her life: "Suddenly, what I thought in the depths of my heart was being told to me by heartless strangers. Just when I was starting to heal up it seemed like the enemy tried to put me down."

Do you have a tender place in the depths of your heart that you are trying to heal up? Is it causing an enormous amount of weariness in your life? You know what? I think most moms can say *yes* to that question. In fact, I'm going to put myself at the front of the line.

My Story

These days, the people I most want to please in life are my kids. I am deeply devastated when I've disappointed them in some way. I worry about the next thing I'll do as a mom that will surely send them to the therapist when they are eighteen. I think, "This time, I'm really going to mess up my girls." Remember my "Fear of failure dominates your life" prediction? I can tell you as a mom, this has been the case more times than I care to admit. A few months ago I was sure I had ruined my daughter's life forever. I should have known better. I could have handled it very differently. I wish I had thought it through, but I didn't.

My oldest daughter just turned fourteen. Last year, she pushed her way into one of the hardest dancing disciplines you can attempt. She learned to dance ballet on pointe. She started dancing at age five and when I saw her achieve her goal of joining a junior dance company and raising her game to pointe level, I was so proud. This challenge did not come without tears. Weekly, she cried when I picked her up from class. We talked a whole lot about perseverance in those days and she conquered her fears, her pain, and her own body. I was not only proud I was inspired. I wrote about her in a book I released during the fall of 2013 called *Being OK with Where You Are*. I asked her if I could share the story, but I published it without letting her read it. When the book arrived from the printer she grabbed a copy and began to read.

I went upstairs to put something away and when I came back down to the kitchen I heard her sobbing in the bathroom. I went to the door and asked her what was wrong. She choked out the answer.

"You told them how much I weighed?" she asked through tears.

"Oh, honey, yes I did. I was trying to be descriptive. I was making the point that you persevered. It is a good thing. Plus, sweetheart, you don't weigh very much at all. Mommy thinks you are just perfect the way you are."

She continued to cry.

I tried to tell her every woman who read the book would wish with all her heart they could be this weight too. She was not too sure about that. Suddenly, in this moment I remembered being her age and having other people laugh at me about my hair. There is nothing worse. I quickly apologized.

She would not come out of the bathroom for anything. I promised to change the text as soon as I could, but it would have to wait a few days until my husband returned from a business trip. She finally came out and I felt swallowed up by the failure and guilt almost immediately.

A few days later, she was able to talk about it. She told me maybe she overreacted a bit and I did not have to change the text. I told her I was sorry I did not let her read it before I sent it to the printer. (Rest assured she has read this story and given it her wholehearted approval.)

Let me tell you what the guilt did in my own heart that week. I concluded I was the worst girl-mom in the world. Who in the world would write down or publish her daughter's weight other than on her actual birthday when it was less than ten pounds? *I should have thought this through. I can't be trusted. She may never heal from the hurt I have caused her. I need to pull the book from the publisher's shelves. In fact, I should quit writing altogether.*

Now, who was the one overreacting a little bit? Maybe, just maybe, I know where she gets her flair for the dramatic. I think I might have thrown myself on my bed, texted a few mommy writer friends, and eaten more than my share of M&M's.

Mommy guilt can cause a weariness a nap won't fix. It weighs us down and wears us out. It turns perfectly normal moms into women who are convinced they could win the prize for *Worst Mom of the Year.* I have spent years reading about and trying to understand grace, and I'm convinced it is the antidote for guilt. The two can't live together. One displaces the other. Ideally, grace lives and breathes in our life, and guilt leaves. But, more often than not the opposite is true. How do we give grace more space to rest in our lives? I think we need to regularly root out the lies we believe, release the guilt, and reclaim our freedom as daughters of Christ.

Root Out the Lies

Webster's Dictionary of 1828 states that a lie is "a falsehood uttered for the purpose of deception." When you believe a lie you are being deceived. It sounds simple, right? But lies are slick, often wrapped in a small element of truth, and connected to other basic lies we are prone to believe. The challenge we face is untangling the mess. Have you ever dug up a tree and moved it to another place in your yard? Well, me neither, but a pastor I once knew had and he said when you do this type of work, you have to dig deep. This gives the tree a chance to start fresh. We need a fresh start, too, as moms. So let's keep this image in mind and do a little digging of our own. Let's see if we can't find the truth in our lives and cut away any lies that are holding us down. We can use my story as an example.

What is the truth? My words legitimately hurt my daughter and this caused me grief.

What is the lie? I'm the worst mom in the world and should quit writing.

The hurt she felt was valid. My remorse for this action was also valid. This truth wrapped around the lie, calling my value as a mom and writer into question, had the potential to become explosive in my life. Left unchecked, the lie would have negated any chance of you reading the book you now hold in your hands. It never would have been written. I'm sure the enemy would have loved for me to quit. He was using this lie to convince me he was worth listening to. He is such a liar. God even says so: "When he lies, he speaks out of his own character, for he is a liar and the father of lies" (John 8:44).

To root out the lie we need to be diligent because the father of lies can be persuasive. It is also important to understand a lie is sometimes connected to other lies we are prone to believe. I heard Beth Moore say once you need to get to the first lie you believe and then untangle all the others. The first lie I am most likely to believe is God does not see me or know what is happening. I feel alone. When I feel this way, I am easily convinced that *I'm the worst mom in the world*. I can choose to be a slave to my emotions or I can root out the lie and move on to the next step. Once bound by the first wave of emotion, I begin to spiral down and believe even more lies. When I move on, I move one step closer to freedom. Doesn't that sound so much better?

Release the Guilt

Guilt is based in the fear you will be defined by *the last mistake you made*. But the grace offered to us in Christ has already redeemed you from your past sins and covers *the next mistake you will make*.

> With the arrival of Jesus, the Messiah, that fateful dilemma is resolved. Those who enter into Christ's being-here-for-us *no longer have to live under a continuous, low-lying black cloud*. A new power is in operation. The Spirit of life in Christ, like a strong wind, has magnificently cleared the air, freeing you from a fated lifetime of brutal tyranny at the hands of sin and death (Romans 8:1-2 MSG, emphasis mine).

What a powerful description of guilt. It hangs in the air and covers us like a black cloud when we make mistakes. And let's face it, as a mother you will make more mistakes. Peyton Manning spoke about something like this when he said, "My faith doesn't make me perfect, it just makes me forgiven."[1]

Likewise, being a Christian does not make you a perfect mother. It means you are forgiven. To walk in the forgiveness we have in Christ still means we need to identify any actual sins related to your actions or words.

- Did you yell at your kids?
- Did you not keep your word to them?
- Did you act selfishly?

If so, one of the most powerful steps to releasing the guilt is to confess your sin to Jesus (which is a churchy way of saying, "I agree with you that I have made a mistake, Lord"). We may also need to say, "I'm sorry. Mommy really blew it," to our kids as well. When we do this we give grace room to breathe and the *spirit of Christ clears the air.* In your humility and honesty Christ will lift you up and guilt will no longer weigh you down.

Keep in mind, not everything you feel guilty about as a mom is necessarily sin. If you look back at the list at the beginning of this chapter, you'll see that many of the responses moms gave are simply choices they feel guilt over. Lysa Terkeurst says in her best-selling book *Unglued,* "Feelings are indicators, not dictators."[2] What are your emotions indicating about your beliefs? Emotions are not always reliable and can point to lies we talked about in the above section. You can release this emotional guilt as well and reclaim your freedom, which is the next step in the process.

Reclaiming Your Freedom

Now that we have identified the lies we believed and released the mommy guilt, it is time to reclaim our freedom by renewing our minds with truth. The only way we are going to make it as moms is to know what God says about us and live out this identity every day. I don't want to overwhelm you with too many words in this section because I want you to be able to remember it quickly. Plus, I know you are probably reading this while cooking dinner, sitting in the car line, or waiting for your son to finish soccer practice. We grab time when we can as moms to renew our minds. Besides, a little bit of truth can gain you a whole lot of freedom. Here are five grace-filled truths you can use to reclaim your freedom as his daughter:

1. **I am deeply loved:** "As the Father has loved me, so have I loved you" (John 15:9).

2. **I know Christ lives in me:** "I have been crucified with Christ. It is no longer I who live, but Christ who lives in me. And the life I now live in the flesh I live by faith in the Son of God, who loved me and gave himself for me" (Galatians 2:20).

3. **I am empowered with everything I need for life and godliness:** "His divine power has granted to us all things that pertain to life and godliness, through the knowledge of him who called us to his own glory and excellence" (2 Peter 1:3).

4. **I believe God is for me:** "If God is for us, who can be against us" (Romans 8:31).

5. **I am victorious:** "But thanks be to God, who in Christ always leads us in triumphal procession, and through us spreads the fragrance of the knowledge of him everywhere" (2 Corinthians 2:14).

One way you could use these five truths is to simply focus on one each day of the week, Monday through Friday. Won't it be wonderful to remember on Monday you are deeply loved and on Friday you are victorious? These truths breathe grace, don't you think? Close your eyes and hear them as words spoken over you by the One John calls "full of truth and grace" (John 1:14). Because they are.

Oh, friend, I know this is not an easy assignment. Living free doesn't happen by accident. It takes intentionality to root out the lies, release the guilt, and reclaim our freedom as daughters in Christ. But the effort it takes to live free is less than the yoke of guilt. Sometimes, like in my case, you get to relearn these lessons more than once. The good news is I'm making progress and moving toward freedom more quickly these days. I'm praying you and I can walk in this freedom together. Remember, guilt has no place in the space of grace. I'll remind you from time to time and be blessed if you do the same for me.

Chapter 6

When Gentle Words Won't Come
Brooke

My youngest son has an amazing laugh.

Everyone who hears it smiles big and tells us the same thing—"he's incredible!"—and I nod my head in agreement, because he is. The only problem is that his laugh drives me, well, batty.

As an introvert, the hardest part about raising two of "those boys" (the ones who are 250 percent boy) is the constant "boy noise," especially when it's in small spaces. I'm convinced that if we lived on two-plus acres of farmland in the country, their noise wouldn't be a problem. I could simply scoot them out the door after school and let them be little boys. Unfortunately, we live on less than half an acre right on the outskirts of our city. We have one semi-climbable tree, and neighbors who we *think* like us in spite of the high decibels coming from our home—but we do not have room for our boys to run and be as loud as they'd like.

I long for this (*long* for it, I say) kind of life for my boys. I want them to run, fall, scrape their knees, build things from scratch, and learn to "rough it." And in spite of our close quarters, I do try to stoke their creative little boy fires as much as possible.

However...

My little rough-and-tumble boys are also fiddlers. Every week we drive almost four hours round trip to take them to violin lessons with the best instructor we can afford, because they have a gift and find great pleasure in playing this instrument. For the first hour or so of the trip, things are usually fine, but just give it enough time and the "big laugh in small spaces phenomenon," as we've come to call it, creeps out and starts to drive mama crazy.

My little guy, whom others see as simply amazing, starts to sound like a hyena on crack...or at least it sounds that way to me.

I've asked, begged, threatened discipline, explained why it's so important to me as the driver that he keep it down, pulled over, driven faster, and thought seriously about never getting in another car with this kid for the rest of my life, but nothing works. (Obviously, since he's six, I have a few more years before I can actually refuse to get in the car with him.)

If it were only a matter of time spent in the car, I would probably be okay. But over time, an immediate physical and emotional response started to occur in me at the sound of his laughter whether we were in the car or not, and I found myself completely unable to tolerate his laughter on any level.

Not good.

I was so annoyed by my son's inability to control the power of his laugh that I was punishing him for even having one.

Imagine that—punishing a child for laughing. Possibly one of my finest mothering moments. Most certainly one of the things my son will tell his wife one day to explain why he's so messed up.

Don't get me wrong, my son needs to learn how to control himself in confined areas so he doesn't drive everyone in his life crazy—we'll keep working on that—but his amazing laugh made it clear that Mama needs to work on her own heart, too. I haven't had many gentle words lately—a problem that rears its ugly head most often when my boys are just being boys...albeit loud ones.

My gentle words usually get lost somewhere between broken closet doors hanging on by a thread and swinging light sabers smacking me in the face by accident. I'm honestly a bit ashamed of how many times I've been angry over the last eight years of my life. On the outside, I'm a grown woman who has her life together. I have a nice house, a hunky husband, and two seriously beautiful, talented little boys. But on the inside, I'm a two-year-old stamping her foot and screaming because she can't get her own way.

All I want is for my boys to obey me. And to be quiet. And to stop wrestling all. the. time. And to put their toys away. And to stop goofing off at the table. And to stop spilling their drinks. And to stop wrinkling their noses at the dinners I work hard to fix for them. And to focus on their schoolwork. And to stop fighting with each other. And to be quiet (did I already say that?).

What I *really* want is for God to touch my heart (and those of my children if he has the time) and take away our tendency to sin. No fight. No marathon. No "just keep swimming!" I want to be done with this *now*. Some days I just want to give up, leave it all to chance, and hope things turn out okay. But several months ago, in a time of deep and intense prayer, God made it clear to me that my boys need someone to fight for them, and he's chosen that person to be me. They need a mom who will refuse to be beaten—a mom who will get up, dust herself off, and cast her net one more time. The bottom line, friends, is that we're not getting out of this without some work.

> My boys need someone to fight for them, and that person needs to be me.

The Motherhood Labor

Motherhood is hard physical labor, sweaty work, manual labor of the most intense kind because it requires more than just body. Turns out it's hard heart labor, too. And when the work doesn't pay off? When the pulling and tugging and coaxing and dragging and pushing and begging and praying don't seem to change things as fast as we'd like, we can be left empty, exhausted, worn down. In times like these, it's easy to let it all out, taking our frustrations out on those we love the most. And when we can't stop the toxic flow that comes up from our hearts and out of our mouths you might see us waving the white flag—wanting to give up the fight.

It reminds me of the story of Peter and the disciples in Luke 5:1-9.

A fisherman, Peter had worked hard all night long trying to catch fish and hadn't caught even one. In those days, I imagine an empty net meant an empty stomach, empty table, empty mouths, and maybe, for Peter, an empty heart. I can almost hear him thinking, "All that work for nothing! Wasted effort, wasted time. I should just quit." Ever felt that way, Mom? Useless? Overlooked? A failure? Me too.

Jesus, in need of a safe place from which to teach the people, caught Peter coming in from the long, hard, dirty night of fruitless work, and asked for a simple favor. The crowds, desperate for a word when the voice of God had been silent in their land for four hundred years, were pressing in all around him, and the fisherman's boat looked like a good place to land. He taught the people from the boat for a time, and then told the weary fisherman, Peter, to cast his net in the deep water once more.

Can you imagine Peter's response? *Wait, what did he just say? I gave him my boat, and now this? He's got to be kidding.* Can you picture him, head in hands, eyes tired from lack of sleep, and heart weary from the weight of failure, answering the man Jesus?

Lord, we have been out here all night. We've worked our fingers to the bone trying to provide for our families, trying to take care of them and give them our best. We've given our all, all night long and it hasn't been enough. We're tired, and we don't want to try again. Not even one more time. But because you seem to be something special, we will. Just this once, and don't ask us to do it again if you please.

You know what happened, right? Peter's choice to blow on the flame of hope one last time nearly sank his boat with success. He knew at once that he had been in the presence of greatness, and knowing it, repented, left his nets, and followed Jesus. I find a lot of strength from Peter's story because there's not a week that goes by when I don't entertain the idea of quitting, at least for a few seconds.

Just this week, I sat back and allowed myself to remember what it was like before we had kids. *Freedom* and *quiet* were words that came to mind. I'd never really failed at anything much before becoming a mom, and I never thought loving someone so much could make me feel so bad. Certainly, there are professions that garner more praise, and pay significantly higher wages. As moms, we're trapped in a long-term assignment that often makes us feel like failures, especially when we can't get our words to behave. But I'm beginning to understand that there is a way to find hope in the mess.

I think our victory, like Peter's, starts with one more cast of the net and a new definition of success.

In my book *How to Control Your Emotions So They Don't Control You: A Mom's Guide to Overcoming*, I explore a biblical model for making what comes out of our hearts, and therefore our mouths, submit to the Word of God. I wrote it specifically for moms, but since it released in 2013, I've heard stories of how moms are using it even to train their children to overcome their emotions.

After all, it's our emotions that cause us to lose our tongues. Luke 6:45 says it this way: "The good person out of the good treasure of his heart produces good, and the evil person out of his evil treasure produces evil, for out of the abundance of the heart his mouth speaks."

What's in our heart comes out. Angry that your kids won't obey? It's going to come out. Frustrated over your lack of finances? It's going to come out. Ticked off that your husband doesn't help around the house? You guessed it, it's going to come out. So the key to changing what comes out is to change what's already in our hearts, and friends, it has to start with admitting our sin.

We can't overcome what we won't confess. Getting angry isn't necessarily a sin, but it *is* sinful to allow our anger to control us, our emotions to drive us, and our feelings to inform our actions and the way we treat those we love. Maybe you don't *feel* like asking God to change the way you feel—I get that, and I've been there. As women, we've been trained to believe that we have a right to our own ings, and we're willing to fight hard to keep them. But the truth that if our feelings are in conflict with the Word of God, they nee to change. Before any significant progress can be made in this area we have to be willing to admit we're wrong and submit our emotions and feelings to the authority of God's Word.

Fact: It is sinful to be controlled by our emotions. God's Word tells us this is 1 Corinthians 6:12: "All things are lawful for me, but I will not be mastered by anything." Certainly, our emotions—the way we feel about every situation we encounter—are lawful, or allowable, even good. Emotions serve as a barometer, helping us access our surroundings and even giving us a glimpse of what's going on in our own hearts, but they shouldn't be given the place of mastery over us. As Christians, the only master of our hearts should be Christ. Anything else allowed to control, dictate, or rule is an idol, and must be dethroned as quickly as possible.

If you've let your emotions run your life, causing you to treat those you love most sinfully, take a moment now to tell God you're sorry for sinning against him, ask for forgiveness, and choose change. Choose hope. This next section will show you how.

Feel, Know, Do

Tucked into all of those magnificent Psalms is one in particular by David that sets the tone for our entire study. We don't know exactly what was happening in David's life when he wrote Psalm 13, but it's safe to assume he felt death was close and very real. Perhaps his emotions threatened to run away while he was running for his life from Saul. Or maybe he wrote this while in exile from his son Absalom. Maybe it was some other danger that made him feel forgotten and alone. Or perhaps the circumstances of this passage don't matter as much as what it tells us about David's heart. If we look hard enough, Psalm 13 will give us a unique pattern for overcoming our emotions that can be richly useful in our own lives. Below, I've broken the passage down for you into three separate parts to make it easier to see.

> [1–2] How long, O LORD? Will you forget me forever? How long will you hide your face from me? How long must I take counsel in my soul and have sorrow in my heart all the day? How long shall my enemy be exalted over me?

> [3–4] Consider and answer me, O LORD my God; light up my eyes, lest I sleep the sleep of death, lest my enemy say, "I have prevailed over him," lest my foes rejoice because I am shaken.

> [5–6] But I have trusted in your steadfast love; my heart shall rejoice in your salvation. I will sing to the LORD, because he has dealt bountifully with me.

Now let's take the verses apart and see if we can unpack their meaning a little bit more.

Verses one and two seem to describe how David felt during whatever event he was living through. It looks to the everyday reader like he felt abandoned, completely alone, and vulnerable to attack. And why not? If this Psalm were truly written while David was running from Saul or Absalom, it only makes sense he would feel these kinds of emotions. Where was God in the midst of his pain? Didn't he see how David was suffering? Didn't he care? I can almost see his feelings escalating to a breaking point, just like mine do, as David told the Lord of all his woes. But then there's a shift…

Verses three and four detour from groaning and desperation and move toward frustration, but not frustration without purpose. When David said, "O LORD my God; light up my eyes" (verse three), it appears he was inviting God to help him understand his emotions. David may have felt vulnerable, but he was asking God to act in these circumstances in a way that brought glory to his name, and in doing so, began the process of reminding himself of what he knew to be true—God had a plan, David was the rightful king, God had answered David in the past and would again, God promised to protect David from Saul, and on and on.

Then finally, in verses five and six, we see a total shift in tone. We started out with a David who felt abandoned by God, moved to a David who invited God into his circumstances, and now have a David who remembered all God had already done for him in the past and trusted him to do the same in the future. He acted on what he knew to be true instead of how he felt. What he did was affected by what he knew.

That's quite a power-packed little Psalm, but it beautifully displays a model for controlling our emotions that I like to call "Feel, Know, Do."

David allowed himself to feel the pain of whatever life event he was in the midst of, but he didn't allow himself to stay there. He knew the only way to truly bless the Lord was to honor him with his whole heart and respond well to whatever life brought him. Here's the model in a little more detail:

Feel: What we see with our eyes (our experiences and circumstances) affects our emotions and causes us to feel a certain way. Our feelings may be right or they may be wrong, but either way, as believers we're called to submit them to the authority of the Word of God.

Know: Our minds remember what we know to be true (the truth of God's Word, who we are in Christ, all that's available to us because we belong to Him, God's many promises, etc.) when we invite God into our circumstances with an open heart.

Do: We act on truth, not on what we can see or what we feel. What we do is affected by what we know.

As David remembered the joy of his salvation, his heart turned from feelings of despair at what he could see happening in his life to feelings of hope and joy at what he knew God could do, and he acted based on this knowledge.

That's how I want to live my life.[1]

Love Given Freely

In spite of this fabulous model for change God's given us in his Word, I still don't always get it right. I mess up and, more often than not, think I'm doing it all wrong. But I'm choosing to fight. I'm giving this battle for their hearts (and mind) everything I have and trusting God to take care of the rest.

These things we're fighting for don't happen overnight. Oh, how I wish they did. Oh, how I wish I could snap my fingers or wiggle my nose back and forth and make their hearts of stone turn to hearts of flesh (Ezekiel 36:26). I wish I could say a magic word and be done with my sin once and for all. But I don't see that principle in the Bible.

Are we overcomers? Yes. Revelation 12:10-11 says so. Are we cleansed from sin, forgiven for our not-so-gentle words if we've placed our faith in Christ? Absolutely! Psalm 103:12 says God has removed our sins from us as far as the east is from the west. This is fabulous news! In the end, we win! But in the meantime, we *keep* overcoming, day-by-day, little-by-little. Over time, small triumphs become substantial treasures.

> Over time, small triumphs become substantial treasures.

I used to feel like a total failure when I lost my gentle words *again*, because surely if I mess up I'm a bad mom, and surely my kid will talk about *that time Mom*…in therapy, right?

Wrong.

Allowing for the work of the Holy Spirit in our heart to change us more into the image of Christ takes time. Certainly, there are people whose lives get intersected with Christ and walk away radically changed, but most of us experience success in small measures. If we mess up there's new mercy for tomorrow. As long as there's a desire to love Jesus more than we love our sin, there's hope for change. *This* is my new definition of success.

Friends, I can't promise that following these steps to Feel, Know, and Do will radically change your life. I know from personal experience that they can, but they only work if you continually confess your sin and use them with intention and determination. I can't promise your next act of obedience will produce the fruit in your children's hearts you've been craving. You can only allow God to change *your* heart, not your child's. I can't promise you that following Christ, even just one more time, will bring immediate change or smashing success. I can't even promise that finding the gentle words today means you'll keep them for tomorrow.

But I can promise that holding out that flicker of hope, just enough to propel your feet forward in one more step of faith, matters to God. He sees you, and he knows what it will require to pursue your heart. He'll pursue it with reckless abandon, just because he loves you that much. But in the same way that he loves you, the same way he'll move all of heaven to chase your heart and make it his, he also loves your children. When they break your heart, they break his. When they run away from you, they run away from him. When they reject your love, they reject his. When they refuse to walk in obedience to you, they refuse to walk in obedience to him. He hurts with you.

But his plans for you—and your children—are good.

In the stillness of the holy moments right before bed, as I lie next to my oldest and see the man he's becoming, I decide to speak love to him. I tell him mama loves his head and his eyes, his ears and his nose, his neck and his chest, his tummy and his arms, his hands and his fingers, his legs and his knees, his feet and his toes. I love every bit of who he is, and I love the strong, mighty, awesome warrior man of God he is becoming. I love his kind heart and I love his protective nature. I love his desire to learn and I love that God has given him the gift of music, all for his glory.

It's a moment of pure divine inspiration—when God allows two hearts, mama and her baby boy (who's not such a baby anymore), to align and speak the heart's language. He glows under the weight of this love, then pauses, thinks, and says,

"I haven't been so awesome…"

His eyes look down as the shame and godly sorrow I've been begging God for come and visit his little heart.

Why is it that love given freely, washed over someone with reckless abandon, does more to change the heart than begging and pleading? I think it's because of the Son. The same Son who was crushed and beaten, who looked into the eyes and hearts of those he had come to save and loved them into repentance.

It's his kindness that leads us to repentance (Romans 2:4). Not his wrath, not his judgment, not his punishment for sin. Kindness.

He gave us Jesus. Jesus, our tabernacle. Jesus, our safe place. Jesus, where we go to find the strength to try one more time.

Will you make a commitment with me today, friend? Can we stand together, unified by Christ and our love for our children, and covenant with the Lord that we will never, ever give up the fight? Can we covenant with the Lord that we will never give up on his ability to move in our hearts and those of our children?

Say it with me…

"I believe God's plans for me are good. Therefore, I commit today that I will never give up on my family, and I will never give up on God's ability to move in our hearts. With his help, I will take the next step of faith even when I don't feel like it, because he is the God of miracles."

I will never give up on my family, and I will never give up on God's ability to move in our hearts.

I believe God will meet us and fill our nets as we trust Him enough to cast our nets just one more time. Will you invite Jesus into your mess right now? He's already there, close by, waiting for you to call. Pray with me?

Jesus, I give this messy life to you. These messy kids, my messy attempts to be what they need, our messy sinful responses to life—I give it all to you. Meet me here in these moments, help me remember that you are what my kids really need and that I have access to you in prayer—both for myself and my kids—to give me the strength I need to keep going. Thank you for hearing when I pray. In Jesus's name, amen.

Chapter 7

When You Want to Run and Hide

Stacey

Mothering is a marathon, but sometimes I don't want to run to win. I want to run away and hide. Why? Because this weary mom is tired. I am bone-deep tired. It is the kind of tired when everything hurts and I can't remember my last name. I have had enough of tired. Do you feel it too? Can you even remember a day in the last year when you didn't feel it? "Lord, give me one good day at the spa and I'll be a new mom," I have whispered. But is it really enough?

I recently spent an afternoon at a spa called *Bonjour*. It was my friend's birthday, and her husband treated us to a day filled with pampering. I have never been so relaxed in my life. After our spa time, we had lunch in a grownup restaurant with real live grownup conversation. I did not have to stop eating to cut up food or take a small person to the potty. I was beginning to put complete sentences together and think clearly for the first time in weeks. Until...

I picked up my three older girls from their Friday enrichment program. While I was at the spa, they were storing up a whole slew of discouragements about their day. As the van door opened, they poured them out simultaneously for me to hear. When we arrived home, the baby added her dissatisfaction at Mommy for leaving her all day as well. Within minutes, everyone wanted to know what I was going to cook for dinner. Later, to add insult to injury, I looked down and noticed my freshly manicured hands were dirty and my Sassy Platinum nail polish had chipped. The happy and relaxed feeling melted away and I was left to think how in the world I could get it back.

Defining Weary

I've always wondered why I had the urge to run away and hide when I was feeling particularly weary. On days when I am not afforded the chance to soak my feet at the Bonjour Spa, I create elaborate escapes in my mind. My escapes usually include a trip to Target because I can shop and get my Starbucks fix at the same time. Which, by the way is genius. Sometimes, I devise a plan to visit Barnes and Noble to eat my favorite vanilla cupcake and read a stack of magazines. The point is, I long to be somewhere else, anywhere but where I am, overwhelmed by all the neediness of the people who live in my home. It is as though I'm being drawn inward and away all at the same time.

Recently, I had an *aha moment* while reading the Bible. Do you know what I'm talking about? This type of moment happens when your life intersects so drastically with truth you feel like there is a light shining down from the heavens on you. In my aha moment, I discovered the Hebrew meaning for the word *weary*.

First of all, I found out there are at least fourteen Hebrew words for *weary*. Included in the list you will find thirteen adjectives describing how weary feels and one verb telling you what weary does. This is a great indication that our one English word probably doesn't fit every real life weary situation. The verb used here perfectly describes this weary mom.

uph: to fly, fly about, fly away[1]

Weary wants to run because running feels right. Not only does it feel right, it is at the core of what it means to be weary. As it turns out, I'm not the only mom who has felt weary and wanted to run away. Other moms have experienced the same desire. I know because I bump into them while waiting for my sugar free vanilla latte. I've read their Facebook status updates. I see it in their eyes at church when they are dropping their kids off for Sunday school. Guess what? I think I may have found the first weary mom runner on the pages of Genesis. Let's meet her and see who she ended up running into.

The First Mama Who Ran

She was a mom in the middle of a dark and desperate situation. Her name was Hagar and she was a housemaid to Sarah, the wife of Abraham. Sarah didn't like Hagar much because she happened to be expecting Abraham's firstborn child. It is a long story, something like an episode of *Days of Our Lives*. The bottom line is that Sarah treated Hagar harshly. Hagar had enough of the abuse, and so she ran until she could not put one foot in front of the other, collapsing in a heap of hurt, tears, and anonymity. Alone in the wilderness she might have wondered what would become of her.

But God had her precisely where he wanted her. Weary and worn, she was in a place where she could hear him speak.

Gently, he spoke her name.

What, you know me?

Firmly, he reminded her of her humble position.

You know the way I take?

Directly, he told her what she was to do.

Is there no other way?

But God did not send her back weary and worn. He had a promise for her to claim as her own.

- A promise of life.
- A promise of a future.
- A promise of mercy.

Thereafter, Hagar used another name to refer to the LORD, who had spoken to her. She said, "You are the God who sees me." She also said, "Have I truly seen the One who sees me?" (Genesis 16:13 NLT).

Here, where she never expected, he met her. He had pursued her heart, not because she deserved it, but because that is who he is—in her words—El Roi, the all-seeing God who sees *me*.

Hiding in Plain Sight

Hagar called God *El Roi* because he saw her. He saw her even though she was trying hard to NOT be seen. I know on the days when I want to run and hide, what I really need is someone to see me. I need someone to see my hurt, to see my struggle, and to tell me it is going to be all right.

El Roi has a word for you and me for days like this. He planted it smack in the middle of a book in the Old Testament. It also happens to be one of my favorite verses. "For the eyes of the LORD move to and fro throughout the earth that He may strongly support those whose heart is completely His" (2 Chronicles 16:9 NASB). See, God knows a thing or two about hiding and seeking. He knows all your good hiding places. He sees you because he is looking intently for you. He scans the whole earth looking with one purpose in mind: He longs to strongly support you. The girl who, when it comes down to it, is completely his anyway.

Have you ever played peek-a-boo with a baby? They squeal with delight when you pretend that you don't know where they are and you "find them." They have no idea they are hiding in plain sight and you have had your eyes on them the whole time. They think in all their baby craftiness they had you fooled. We know the truth. Silly babies, you can't hide from your mama.

When we try to run and hide from our heavenly Father, it is the same thing. We may think in all our big girl craftiness we are hiding from him. But El Roi is the all-seeing God. We can't find a Starbucks out of his sight or a mall he doesn't know about. We really can't go unseen from his all-seeing eyes.

The Best Place to Run and Hide

◇◇◇◇◇◇◇◇◇◇◇◇◇◇◇◇◇◇◇◇◇◇◇◇◇◇◇◇◇◇◇◇

Rock of ages, cleft for me, let me hide myself in thee.
—Augustus Montague Toplady

◇◇◇◇◇◇◇◇◇◇◇◇◇◇◇◇◇◇◇◇◇◇◇◇◇◇◇◇◇◇◇◇

If hopelessness had a day, it was when they placed the body of Jesus in a tomb and rolled the stone in place. Most of his followers hid that day. Who could blame them? I probably would have been right in the middle of the crew of eleven in the upper room that day.

But Mary Magdalene did not hide. Instead she went to where she knew Jesus could be found. Mark 16 tells us she and other women went to anoint the body for a proper burial, but I think she went for different reasons as well. I believe she went to pour out not only oil, but her desperate heart. Broken and honest, she began to weep before the empty tomb (John 20). What a picture, right? It is so like us. We fall down before him and think he is nowhere to be found, when really he is about to move in a way we could never imagine.

Jesus spoke her name. She knew it was him. He met her in the middle of her sorrow and she was never the same. That day, Mary became the first grace clinger. She did not want to let him go. She saw with her own eyes that running to Jesus always brings about a miracle.

> She saw with her own eyes that running to Jesus always brings about a miracle.

When we cling to Jesus he does a miracle in our lives too. We need to come to a point where we believe along with Mary that hiding anywhere away from Jesus is never going to result in victory in our lives. As moms, when we run and hide from the calling he has placed on us, we are really running and hiding from our source of strength—Jesus. He said, "Come to me, all of you who are weary and carry heavy burdens, and I will give you rest" (Matthew 11:28 NLT).

We don't really want a mocha frappe when we are weary. What we really want is rest for our weary souls. Mamas, we have got to get into the habit of running to him and not from him. And honestly, I'm speaking to this mama first.

We Run to a Throne of Grace

What does running to Jesus on our darkest days look like? I'd love to leave you with a strong visual cue for the days when you just have to run somewhere.

In the movie *One Night with the King* Hollywood tells the story of Esther, a Hebrew orphan girl who ends up Queen of Persia. Esther is one of only two books in the Bible that bears the name of a woman. And girls, she is the kind of woman we can look to when learning how to run to and not from God.

This movie is in no way completely accurate to the biblical text, but it does a pretty good job of storytelling. My favorite part is toward the end when Esther enters the king's presence without permission in order save her people, the Hebrews. If the king does not extend his scepter to her she will be instantly killed for coming into his courts uninvited. On the other hand if she doesn't risk her life in this way, she and her people will die as a result of a law he was tricked into signing.

> She runs for her life and for the lives of those she loves. Running past the outer courts through the rain, she throws open the large ornate doors with all her might. The inner court is scattered with a few select nobles. She does not see them. Her eyes are downcast, and her heart is set on the one who is seated on the throne. Her presence there is surprising to most. Who told her she could approach with such determination? Does the King know she is there? Confidently she makes her way and stays her course. This is her destiny. She

will die either way—unless he shows mercy. But will he?
When her eyes meet his, her king's, will she see grace sitting
on the throne?

This is how we are to approach Jesus, our King. We run to him. Our hearts are set on him. We approach with staggering confidence. We claim his promise for our weary and overwhelmed hearts. And as our eyes meet his, we see that grace is indeed sitting on the throne.

"So let us come boldly to the throne of our gracious God. There we will receive his mercy, and we will find grace to help us when we need it most" (Hebrews 4:16 NLT).

You know what I think? I think Esther's eyes were really fixed on a throne of grace—far beyond the throne of her husband, the King of Persia. I think she was running to her Savior God, whom she knew would rescue his people. She was claiming his countless promises. She was counting on grace.

When was the last time you ran to the throne of grace with fearless confidence in the One who sits there? Do you need to take grace by the hand and not let go? When was the last time, you took Hebrews 4:16 to heart?

Practically Speaking

My day is spent in active engagement of meeting the needs of my family and loving them well. It is dirty. It is stressful. It is busy. And most days, it is incredibly wearying. The rewards and blessings are not always apparent. So I get run down. I need a break from time to time, and it is welcome.

What are some practical ways a weary mom can refresh and recharge her spirit on a daily basis? I think it is critical for us to take breaks and find time for ourselves even on plain old Tuesday. Here are a few things I do and you might try as well:

1. **Get up 15 minutes early.** I know what you are thinking. "I'm a weary mom and you want me to get less sleep?"

Yes, I do. But we're only talking about 15 minutes, and really when you think about it, that is not a whole lot of time. What do I suggest you do with those 15 minutes? Get a cup of coffee, your Bible, and a journal and start your day with the Lord. Read a verse or two, write out a prayer, and let God help prepare your heart for the day. I started doing this when my oldest was two. I can't tell you how much more smoothly mornings go for this non-morning-loving mama. Just try it. I think you might even add a few more minutes to your morning quiet time—you will love it that much!

2. **Get outside.** Take your kids to the park. Challenge them to a swing-off. I bought an inexpensive box of sidewalk chalk for my girls and on the really hard days, we go outside and they color the driveway beautiful. Walk around the neighborhood alone if your husband or a friend can watch the kids. Being outside can change your perspective in an instant.

3. **Play some tunes.** I find on the really tough days, if I play my favorite worship album while I cook, clean, or drive, I am encouraged and my kids get to hear me singing instead of yelling. This is such a better deal for them.

4. **Make a cup of tea.** This is fairly new for me, but I have to tell you, even though I am extremely committed to my coffee cup, putting the tea kettle on and steeping a spot of tea soothes my soul.

5. **Laugh every day.** Laugh at yourself. Laugh with your kids. Bring the joy back into your home in some way.

6. **Memorize Scripture.** This is probably one of the quickest ways to refresh my mind. I have recently added an amazing app to my phone called *Scripture Typer* which quizzes you on each verse you put on your list

to memorize. It becomes a game you want to beat and all the while you are hiding God's Word in your heart. Win-win.

7. **Give yourself a Mommy time-out**. When my kids were younger, I gave them room time every day. I would put a secure baby gate at their door and pull out their books and toys and let them play alone for 20 minutes or so. Now that they are bigger, I put myself in time-out daily in my room. I may do a chore, exercise, take a power nap, or write during this time. But for at least 20 minutes I slip away by myself. This is absolutely vital for this weary mom.

8. **Read a classic.** Last May I was completely drained of every thought, emotion, and word I had in my head. I decided what I needed was a good book. Having never read *Pride and Prejudice* by Jane Austen, I quickly downloaded it for free on my Kindle reader. I read it in about four days. Somewhere in the reading of this classic story, I discovered I was in fact human and I could mother small humans again. So many classic books are free now—if not for your Kindle reader, pick it up at your local library.

9. **Take a bath.** This is my favorite time of day. I don't worry about it being fancy, but you certainly can light a candle, play some music, and drink your tea while you soak. Just make sure the kids are in bed or they are being supervised. Take it from me, when you soak in the tub you might just fall asleep.

10. **Invest in something you love to do.** Do you like to take photographs, bake, run, paint, or dance? Whatever it may be, take time every day to do something that makes your heart come alive. Don't forget who God made you

to be. For me these things include writing, blogging, and singing. I try to find time in my crazy schedule to develop these loves of mine as well as raising the kids my heart loves. What do you love to do?

Meanwhile, Back at the Spa

As wonderful and needed as my day at the spa was, I know I can't live there. My reality as a mom is quite different. The benefits of these breaks only go so far. What is the answer for a mom who is daily poured out? How does even the most determined woman of faith not give sway to being overwhelmed? I'm pretty sure I found it here:

> Have you never heard? Have you never understood? The LORD is the everlasting God, the Creator of all the earth. He never grows weak or weary. No one can measure the depths of his understanding (Isaiah 40:28 NLT).

Jesus understood a life poured out. Jesus knew dirty, busy, and tired. He had twelve men pressing hard upon him every single day to love them well. He also knew the pressure of the sick and hurting and of the masses. When he grew tired, he knew where to go. He knew his Father would not grow weary. The Bible tells us "Jesus often withdrew to the wilderness for prayer" (Luke 5:16 NLT). He prayed. He withdrew to the wilderness. He spoke to his Father. Often. And in doing so, he also left us an example of what we are to do when we find ourselves in the midst of the wearying life as a mom. His promise in Isaiah continues:

> He gives power to the weak and strength to the powerless. Even youths will become weak and tired, and young men will fall in exhaustion. But those who trust in the Lord will find new strength. They will soar high

on wings like eagles. They will run and not grow weary.
They will walk and not faint (Isaiah 40:29-31 NLT).

Are you weak? Do you need strength to get up and cook dinner? Are you tired? Moms who put their trust in the Lord have the
promise of new strength and hope that will soar like eagles in their
hearts. Sassy Platinum nail polish can't do that. The only hope we
have is a life of complete dependence upon our Father. He sees us
with all-seeing eyes, understands us completely, and wants to meet
us in the middle of our mess and rescue us from hopelessness. He
sent us Jesus to show us the way home with hope.

Chapter 8

When Life Hurts Too Much

Brooke

There's a box in my room. A recipe box. Blue. Translucent. Etched in cheap silver metal. And it stayed closed for over six months.

When I bought the box my heart was filled with dreams. Overflowing with hope for the future and faith in a God of miracles, I wrote the names of my loved ones on index cards and tucked them away there for safe-keeping. My secret prayers.

The box symbolized a season of new faith in God's Word, God's love, and the power of prayer. Challenged to believe in a God who could and would meet all of my needs according to his riches in Christ Jesus, I hand-selected private prayers for each of the people I love most in this world.

For a month I faithfully prayed for God to help my boys love to read. I joyfully pleaded with him to provide us with a car (after I wrecked the one we had). I wholeheartedly believed in his ability to bring healing to my loved ones and provide for their needs. And I petitioned him to breathe life, and health, and peace into the heart of the tiny baby I carried next to my heart—the baby whose very presence filled me with excitement, dread, hope, and fear—all at the same time.

In early September of 2011 we went in to the obstetrician's office for a regular seven-week maternity check-up. I had been feeling much worse with this pregnancy than with either of the two before it. I was drained and nauseous as we waited to be seen, and remember telling my OB that the morning sickness just felt worse this time. He joked and said it was probably because I had two other small children to take care of. I thought he was probably right.

We made our way to the ultrasound room, prepared to meet our newest addition for the first time. However, it was apparent to me within the first few moments that something was wrong. After several twists of the wand and pushes of the button, the sonographer, a friend of ours, turned to me with tears in her eyes and broke the news: This baby was no longer with us.

On September 20, 2011, our third child slipped from my womb into eternity with God, and I closed the lid to my prayer box.

Closing the Lid

The day we lost our baby, I closed the lid on my dreams and locked away my secret prayers for him inside a cheap blue recipe box. My closest friends and my precious husband took good care of me, and God continued to provide for my needs, even answering the desire of my heart to miscarry naturally. There were constant signs of his love and care for us during that season of loss, but a part of my heart closed that day with the box. I put away my dream of having three boys, embraced all the good God had already given me, and closed the lid.

To those around me, I appeared to be managing the grief well. But the depth of my prayer life took a hit, and a pervasive cynicism crept into my heart, replacing my faith in the God who could move mountains. I was shaken, and no longer sure God would come when I called.

I imagine Mary must have felt a bit like that when Jesus finally came to her after Lazarus's death.

We first learn about Mary through the famous (or infamous) story of Mary and Martha in Luke 10:38-42.

> Now as they went on their way, Jesus entered a village. And a woman named Martha welcomed him into her house. And she had a sister called Mary, who sat at the Lord's feet and listened to his teaching. But Martha was distracted with much serving. And she went up to him and said, "Lord, do you not care that my sister has left me to serve alone? Tell her then to help me." But the Lord answered her, "Martha, Martha, you are anxious and troubled about many things, but one thing is necessary. Mary has chosen the good portion, which will not be taken away from her."

Mary was the one who sat at Jesus's feet while he taught. She wanted to be near him, hear him, love him, and learn from him. She's the relater to Martha's doer, and yet all that changed when her brother, Lazarus, died. I've read the story of Mary, Martha, and Lazarus many times. If you've spent any time in church at all, you likely have too. But there's a small piece of the story I had managed to somehow overlook all these years. Small, but powerful when we're learning to trust again.

Her family had sent word to Jesus four days prior that their brother was sick and needed the Savior's attention, but he hadn't come. By the time Jesus arrived, Lazarus's body had already started to rot, and in Mary's eyes, all hope for his life was gone. Mary, who had once so eagerly embraced Jesus, felt abandoned by the man she once believed could do anything. Here's the little verse that had escaped my attention for so long…

> So when Martha heard that Jesus was coming, she went and met him, but Mary remained seated in the house (John 11:20).

Maybe it's because the doer in Martha wouldn't allow her to neglect something that needed to be done. Or maybe, because doers don't thrive on relationships the way relaters do, Jesus's absence during her time of need didn't hurt her as much. Whatever the reason, Martha went to Jesus when he arrived even though Lazarus was already dead. But Mary, the one Jesus once praised for sitting at his feet, the one who neglected serving to share in the Master's teaching, the one who opened her heart to Jesus so deeply, now sat unmoved by his presence.

Why?

I believe it was because she no longer trusted him with her heart. Matthew Henry states that Mary "was so overwhelmed with sorrow that she did not care to stir, choosing rather to indulge her sorrow, and to sit poring upon her affliction, and saying, *I do well to mourn.*"[1]

I Do Well to Mourn

Mary had lost heart, and while Scripture doesn't give us an inside look at exactly what she felt, it's easy to deduce she felt abandoned, alone, and angry with her Jesus. I felt each of those emotions in the wake of my miscarriage. Maybe you've felt them associated with a different kind of loss in your life. I still believed God was good, but I closed off the place of radical belief in his desire to be good *to me*. I quit dreaming. Quit hoping. And just sat still, basking in what goodness he had already given, refusing to dream that he might give it again. For someone who's a natural dreamer, that's a pretty big deal.

My radical faith had gone into mourning.

Within a six-year time period, my family lost two favorite uncles, a grandfather, a grandmother, a favorite aunt, and a child. My husband was a first responder to the Virginia Tech shootings. He worked inside of Norris Hall before it was cleaned up, wondering which classroom held the memory of our friend killed there that day. Six people in six years caused me to walk a bit more tentatively, wondering what I might lose next.

I hugged more slowly, kissed more deeply, cherished more freely.

But that much grief changed me. My heart was constantly waiting for the next sucker-punch of life.

Loss changes everything.

Maybe the lid to my prayer box had been slowly closing all that time, and the miscarriage locked it. After living a fairly uneventful life, losing six people in six years nearly did me in. Add to that the disciplines of daily life, homeschooling two rambunctious boys also born in that season of loss, and dealing with the stress of a husband who works shift-work, and you get an ugly but clear picture of all that lurked beneath the surface of my heart, just waiting for whatever it took to put me over the edge.

It was a difficult but necessary place for me to dwell, because losing so much in such a short span of time forced me to ask the tough questions about life. I looked deeply at the cross, and wondered, *If God never answered another prayer for me, if he never met another need, would his gift of Jesus and my salvation be enough?* I wasn't sure.

Seasons of Grief

I sat in church one Sunday soon after my miscarriage surrounded by babies. Some were newborns, others yet-to-be-borns, but none of them were mine. I closed my eyes to drown out the sights and realized my hand rested gently on my stomach.

Consciously or unconsciously, women all over the world rest their hands on their tummies as if to speak to, comfort, or reassure the life they carry within. I did it too that day, even though the life inside of me had been gone for two months. As if placing my hand over my stomach could somehow connect me with the life I'd lost, I held it there and whispered, "*I miss you.*"

If someone had handed me a baby I would've lost control. No one did. Instead, I sat on the pew surrounded by friends, but still completely alone, wondering if they had any idea of the effect their joy was having on my pain. In fact, the pain had taken me by surprise. I wasn't prepared to feel the loss of my little one so keenly that day. Life had gone on. Grief tended to find me in unexpected places, and I had done my best to move into it, feel it, and keep walking forward.

But let's be honest. It's in times like these that all we really want to do is turn around and walk away.

When life hurts too much, we desperately search for a way out, clawing away from the point of pain. Pain, by definition, hurts, makes us uncomfortable, and changes our perspective, and I've found that pain, disappointment, and challenge tend to make me question the God who made me.

Do you not see me? Do you not love me?

Why? Why would we choose to follow a God who allows our pain? Why give our hearts to a God who doesn't always answer our desperate prayers the way we think is best? Why serve a God who allows our children to die, our spouses to get sick, our houses to burn, and our kingdoms to fall?

Why Are We Serving God?

The crowds followed Jesus closely as he healed their sick, made their lame walk, and made life and breath and being enter back into their dead. He had filled their stomachs with bread, met their needs, made their spirits soar as he fulfilled his calling from Isaiah 61 to bind up the brokenhearted and release the captives. But the tone of the conversation changed in John 6 as Jesus began to reveal the real reason he had come and question why they were following him.

"Truly, truly, I say to you, you are seeking me, not because you saw signs, but because you ate your fill of the loaves" (John 6:26).

Why do you seek him? Why do I? With these words, Jesus begins to draw the line in the sand. "Why do you love me?" he says. "Why are you following me? Is it because of what I can do for you, how I can meet your needs, or provide what you want? Or do you really love me for who I AM?"

"After this many of the disciples turned back and no longer

walked with him. So Jesus said to the Twelve, 'Do you want to go away as well?'" (John 6:66-67).

When life hurts too much, many turn back from following Jesus and walk with him no longer. I've felt the pull to walk away. I've questioned God's goodness, felt an icy grip on the edges of my heart as I begin to wonder if he really cares about his children, about me.

> If I turn away from Jesus, where will I go?

But the question that always stops me is this: If I turn away from Jesus, where will I go?

Jesus, who died for me while I was in the midst of sinning. Jesus, who gave his life as a ransom for mine. Jesus, who paid the penalty I deserved to pay. His back laid open should have been mine. His face bruised and battered should have been mine. His blood spilled should have been mine. I should have been called a traitor, my integrity questioned. I should have been publicly ridiculed for my sin, my attempts at being God tried before a jury of my peers. I should have died with the weight of my sin upon my shoulders, God's hand of wrath on my head.

He took it all.

> Simon Peter answered him, "Lord, to whom shall we go? You have the words of eternal life, and we have believed, and have come to know that you are the Holy One of God" (John 6:68-69).

There comes a time in the life of every believer when we must choose to turn away or follow Jesus no matter what, because we know He holds the words of eternal life. He is the Holy One of God. And that's all that matters.

Why do we seek Him? Is it so he can perform for us, take care of all our needs, bind up our wounds, raise our dead? He is that God. He *sees* us. But if we only follow him because of what he does, there will come a time when we feel like he doesn't. Then we must choose if we will turn away or follow him through the difficult times because of **who he is**—the God who bends down to listen (Psalm 116:2).

Hope Is a Choice

During my season of grief, I often felt like God wasn't there—like he didn't see me, didn't hear my prayers, didn't care. But if you look closely, the Bible says all of those feelings I had were wrong. It doesn't negate my feelings to know they're wrong—I very much felt alone, and unheard, even a bit unloved. The Bible simply tells me a different story.

God loves me, hears me, sees me, and yes, is fighting for me, even if I can't see it. I believe it's true because God's Word says it's true, and it's that simple truth that kept me from staying in a place of perpetual hopelessness.

Weariness, depression, pain, desperation—they're all feelings. Though they're in no way invalid, feelings can lie to us, making us see the world around us through a fog so thick we have to claw to find our way out. How much better to choose the hope God offers in his Word.

It might look something like this:

No! God's Word says I'm not alone. He is my ever-present help in trouble, and he'll never leave me. I know he's with me because it's his very nature to be "God with us," and he'll never go against who he is. He hears me, sees me, loves me, and cares for me...even if I don't feel like it's true.

Hope comes from a deliberate, intentional, and focused attempt to believe what God says is true, is true, regardless of what we see around us. It's something we have to fight for—clinging desperately to the truth of God's Word when the fog of our emotions makes it hard to see. But when we make the effort, when we finally say, "I choose hope!" we make room in our hearts for the best kind of healing...

Healing

Slowly but surely my heart returned to Jesus. So did Mary's.

> When [Martha] had said this, she went and called her sister Mary, saying in private, "The Teacher is here and is calling for you." And when she heard it, she rose quickly and went to him...Now when Mary came to where Jesus was and saw him, she fell at his feet, saying to him, "Lord, if you had been here, my brother would not have died."

Jesus called Mary by name. How profound that the Master would know she was missing. The one who sat tenderly at his feet, hanging on his every word, didn't come, so he called for her. And somehow, Mary mustered enough strength to place her hope in Jesus one more time. Maybe all it took was hearing that her name mattered to him to make her get up and run. And even though her first words seemed to accuse him of neglect, we can't overlook the fact that she ran to him at all. Even in the midst of her pain, when she realized he was calling her by name, she went running.

So did I.

I stared at that blue box on my bedroom floor knowing what I had to do, and for the first time in over six months I knew I could do it. There, on the top of the pile of my secret prayers, was a card that simply said, *Baby McGlothlin*. I literally felt as though my heart sighed in relief as I picked it up and turned it over again and again in my trembling hands, knowing Jesus had called me by name.

On a breezy, beautiful day, my family and I drove to a nearby lake. With the glorious water all around us and the sun making us want to jump in, we took the pieces of our dream and released them. I watched the wind take the bits of paper into the water and finally felt at peace with the Lord.

Restoration

We live in a world where speed is everything and waiting is unthinkable. We want what we want, and we want it yesterday. Healing is no different. The world doesn't stop for us to grieve. There are still bills to pay, laundry to do, homework to finish, meals to cook, children to parent. We have to keep living.

But healing can't be forced. It simply takes time. And as with everything else in life, true healing comes as God leads us toward it, peeling back layer after layer of raw hurt and breathing new life into our wounds.

Later in John, as Jesus inches closer and closer to his fate on the cross, we find him once again taking respite in the home of Mary and Martha.

> Six days before the Passover, Jesus therefore came to Bethany, where Lazarus was, whom Jesus had raised from the dead. So they gave a dinner for him there. Martha served, and Lazarus was one of those reclining with him at table. Mary therefore took a pound of expensive ointment made from pure nard, and anointed the feet of Jesus and wiped his feet with her hair. The house was filled with the fragrance of the perfume (John 12:3).

From withholding her heart to offering Jesus the very best she had, Mary now humbles herself and expresses her love and gratitude toward him who could raise the dead. Assured now of his love for her, she shows Jesus just how much she loves him and wipes his dirty, grimy feet with her own hair.

How precious he was to her, this man who had restored her family, restored her heart. Once closed to Jesus because of what she interpreted as neglect, abandonment, and pain, her heart was now fully open to him as her King. I like to think that as Mary poured the expensive ointment over Jesus's beautiful but dirty feet, she also poured out all of the hurts and disappointments she had carried in her heart and entrusted them to her Savior once again. She opened the lid of her heart and walked in faith one more time.

Friend, are there areas of your heart that you've closed off to the Lord? Areas that are just too painful, too disappointing, too devastating to open back up? Have you stopped hoping? Stopped praying? Stopped dreaming about what could be because the lid is closed and locked tight on your heart?

I think Jesus might be calling your name, sweet one. I think he might be inviting you to take the first step back to him and welcoming you to pour out your hurts and disappointments so he can show you who he truly is.

Open the Lid?

I polled women who have suffered a pregnancy loss to find out what practical, tangible, meaningful ways they've employed to open the lid to their grief and celebrate, mourn, and release the lives of their lost children. If you're still in the midst of your loss, whether it happened recently or many years ago, I hope you'll find peace and closure in these suggestions from their hearts to yours.

Jessica

We named each of our babies we lost and, at least between my husband, myself, and a few close friends, we refer to them by their names and not just as the first or second miscarriage. I have a necklace I wear often with the initials of all of my kids.

Also, just allowing myself to be sad when I'm sad about it and not feel like I need to hide it or get over it. They're still my children and I can still miss them. And being able to talk openly with others helps too. I've also found that I'm more comfortable and open to talk with other moms who have lost babies than I originally thought I would be. In a way, I'm eager to because it's shared pain, shared burden, and you don't have to explain the million different, and sometimes contradicting, emotions you feel.

Amber

We named him Samuel and I wear his birthstone along with his siblings' on a necklace.

Joanne

My first pregnancy was a miscarriage at ten weeks. We had just announced the pregnancy to everyone. We sent out an e-mail to share our now sad news. We also e-mailed our prayer chain at church. A few days later we received a beautiful letter from a woman in our church sharing her experience with miscarriage. She helped me so much with my grief. I now have three beautiful boys. When I hear of someone with a miscarriage or loss I always send a note of prayer.

Kim

I found worship music to be a balm to my grieving soul. It helped me gain a greater/wider perspective of God and his abundant love for me.

Rebecca

I wore a ring with tiny footprints on it. Inside the ring it said *It was then that I carried you*, which is a quote from the "footprints in the sand" poem. I felt the phrase had dual meaning to me. I also have a small memory box with the ultrasound pictures and a onesie.

Heather

We adopted a child through sponsorship in honor of each of the three little ones I lost in pregnancy.

Amy

I remember seeking God earnestly in prayer after that loss, and also being able to talk to several close friends who just listened while I poured out my heart helped me so much.

Alexandrea

At first I dismissed the thought of a support group, but just talking through it and realizing it's okay to feel a million different conflicting emotions…it's been helpful beyond words.

Lindsey

Write about it. Release balloons in their honor.

Shelley

Sharing my experience with someone in my family that also suffered a miscarriage. I sent an e-mail because after I had my miscarriage I did not want to talk to anyone. That's why I reached out through an e-mail. I shared all the feelings for myself and my husband. Our child would have been two next month. You never forget.

Peggy

Keeping a daily journal of the thoughts/emotions I was experiencing. I was free to pour my heart out—good, bad, or ugly—and it was okay.

Barb

We named our lost baby girl and we have a special Christmas tree ornament put on our tree each year in her memory.

Valerie

After we lost our first pregnancy, we sponsored a little girl through Compassion International in her memory. We still sponsor her; she lives in the mountains of Peru.

Melissa

The thing that helped (and it really did even though it sounds strange) was becoming a volunteer in the NICU. There was just something about rocking those tiny babies that soothed my spirit.

There would be days that I would sit there and silent tears would run down my face but when I left it felt as though a weight had been lifted even if just for a moment.

Joy

We lost our twin boys when I was 22 weeks pregnant around 12 years ago. We do a balloon release every year on their birthday, we planted a tree in our backyard with a memorial plaque in front of it, they have engraved ornaments on our Christmas tree, I have two angel charms on my mom necklace and Pandora bracelet, and I made a scrapbook of all of their ultrasound pictures.

Lesley

For me, helping others helps me pay tribute to my child.

Cathy

My son was stillborn at 33 weeks. He would have been 11 this year. When dealing with loss of any kind you should allow yourself to grieve and not rush to get back to "normal." Don't allow others to tell you how you should feel. I celebrate his life by hugging his brother and sisters a little tighter.

Lisa

I bought a rock in the shape of a pretty heart. It is pink for the girl I would have had. I have it sitting in a jar on my kitchen counter so I can see it all the time. It's in with other rocks so it is decorative. Also I added a tiny heart to a tattoo I have. You have to know what you are looking for to see it so it's just there for me and my hubby.

Sarah

I bought a birthstone ring. I bought the stone for the due date (rather than the month of loss).

Kristen

Nurses in our hometown started a foundation and purchased a burial plot for pregnancy loss, coordinated with pathology labs and funeral homes—literally did everything. I was absolutely blown away—it met a need I didn't know I had, and was truly significant.

Tracie

I framed the ultrasound in a frame that says "image of an angel." Seeing that and still having it displayed today helps me heal. Basically, being able to mourn openly and celebrate her tiny life, instead of it being something that never happened (because she wasn't born), helped me heal.

Fran

Sending lanterns into the sky helped me put a picture to loss. Also decorating her headstone, talking with other loss moms, and mostly giving back to the hospital in her name (donating parking passes for other NICU parents/memory boxes).

Steps to Opening the Lid

1. Tell Jesus and a trusted friend how much you're hurting. Be honest about where you are and how you're struggling. Tell the truth and allow Jesus to meet your needs. He's waiting.

2. Invite Jesus to get in your mess with you. It's his specialty, and he longs for the opportunity to make even the worst of circumstances birth something beautiful in your life. Tell him it's okay to come on in and get his hands dirty cleaning you up.

3. Talk to Jesus on a regular basis. Call out to him for relief in the midst of your pain. Ask him to show you how to put one foot in front of the other and how to deal with

hard situations you encounter. Beg him for comfort, but know that one of the things he likes to do most is use other people to comfort his children. Open your heart to the idea that others might be sent from him to ease your pain.

4. Stay in his Word. Refuse to allow the pain of your circumstances to keep you away from your source of hope (Romans 15:4) because it's where true healing originates.

5. Choose ways to make your healing tangible. Maybe it looks like one of the stories shared above. Maybe you resonate with what my family did to commemorate the life of our child and release him to the Lord. Whatever you do, do something, even if you have to do it alone. God sees your pain and will validate your grief, because your pain is his pain. He loves you so much, cares so deeply about the pain you encounter in this life, that he sent his only Son to make a way for you to come to him for forgiveness and relief. Come.

Chapter 9

When the World Presses In

Brooke

Most of the stories you've heard so far in this book fall into the category of the everyday weariness all moms experience from time to time. But there are moms who experience a weariness that goes far beyond the ordinary. As we planned for this book, Stacey and I felt it was so very important to find a way to bring hope to that mom, too. So we prayed and asked God if there was someone we could ask to share her personal testimony of God's grace in a mess that goes much deeper than what either of us has ever experienced.

After turning down an interview with Oprah Winfrey, my friend Tracey graciously allowed me the honor of talking to her about "the mess" of losing her only son. Her prayer is that her story might bring you comfort and help you place your hope in the God who met her there.

Her story, and mine, starts in a small town...

Narrows is a sleepy little town in southwestern Virginia. Known for its love of football and people, Narrows is home to a long stretch of the New River—the world's third oldest river geologically speaking, and one of only a few rivers in the world that flows north instead of south. There is one stoplight regulating traffic out of Narrows, one fast food restaurant, one amazing mom and pop restaurant called Anna's, one grade school, one middle school, and one high school. We are the mighty Greenwave, and please don't put an *s* on the end to make us plural. We are one.

In a small town, everyone knows everyone else. Sometimes this is a good thing, and sometimes it's not, but most of the time, the feeling of knowing and being known helps you bypass any hard feelings about it. If you make a mistake in Narrows, most of the community knows about it in time to discuss it over breakfast the next morning. They'll have opinions about what you did and say things like, "her poor mama," or "bless her heart," but they'll also be the first ones to put their arms around you when you go to the altar to repent on Sunday morning.

The churches in Narrows are like extended family. There's one Baptist church, one Methodist, one Disciples of Christ, and a few others located throughout town, but by and large the community lives out life together. Your friends across the river won't end up in a different school district from you, and you certainly won't have to play against them in football. My daddy probably played ball with yours in school, and my mama hosted the Circle meetings of First Baptist for yours once a year.

Overall, it's a peaceful, beautiful little town. Nothing ever happens much in or to the people of Narrows.

Until one day it did.

It was a blustery Monday morning on April 16, 2007. Snow flurries found their way to southwestern Virginia on a day that should have been filled with spring warmth. Students wrapped up in coats crossed the Drillfield at Virginia Tech, pulled into parking spaces, said goodbye to friends, and sat down in their desks to learn, just like any other day.

Tracey Lane, a long time resident of Narrows, got up, fixed breakfast, and went to work in nearby Pulaski, Virginia. She still felt the high of the beautiful weekend she'd just had with her family. They'd gotten the great news that her son, Jarrett, had gotten a teaching assistant scholarship at Florida State University in the engineering department, and that news significantly eased the financial burden of Jarrett's education, something she'd been worrying about for some time.

The day before, Jarrett responded to an altar call at First Baptist Church, and proudly told the congregation about the way God had provided for him, publicly thanking God for taking such good care of his children.

Tracey was so proud of all he'd become.

She thought back to what they had survived as a family—the divorce of her parents, her own divorce, the death of her older brother and two step-siblings—and felt like maybe they were finally hitting their stride. She said a silent *Thank you, God,* and then went to work.

Sometime that morning, Tracey heard the news of a shooting at Virginia Tech, where Jarrett was attending college. Some friends encouraged her to call and check on Jarrett, and she did, but felt sure he was safe even when she couldn't reach him. She thought to herself, "Surely he went back to his apartment after the shooting and is waiting it out like everyone else."

She left him a message and went back to work.

Later, after hours of not being able to reach him, Tracey began to worry. The only man in the family, it was unlike Jarrett to leave his mom and two sisters hanging. She knew him well enough to know that if he were safe, he would want her to know. Visions of him being in the hospital, helping the wounded, or in a room somewhere with survivors began to fill her head, and she told her boss she was going home. She prayed for his safety the whole way.

After her daughters tried with no luck to locate Jarrett in one of the three surrounding hospitals, Tracey knew of only one thing she could do. She grabbed her purse, opened her front door, and ran smack into her family's deacon from First Baptist Church. She looked at him and said, "I'm going to find my baby." His reply? "I'm taking you."

         ⌐~⌐

I picked up my two-year-old from the sitter and planted myself in front of the TV after work, much like every other person in the world that day. My cell phone rang again and I picked it up quickly thinking it was my husband, who had been on campus all day as a part of the emergency response team. It wasn't. It was his brother. "Have you heard from your husband? Can you reach him? Does he know who's dead? Tracey Lane hasn't been able to reach Jarrett all day and he had class in that building this morning. Is there anything he can do to find out?"

I promised to do my best to contact my husband and hit the *end* button on my phone. But before I could even dial his number, my cell phone rang again…

"Tracey just got word. Jarrett is dead."

         ⌐~⌐

Just after 7:15 on the morning of April 16, 2007, two students were shot to death inside West Ambler Johnson Hall. Approximately two hours later, all the way across campus, Seung-Hui Cho barricaded the doors of Norris Hall and began a killing spree that would take the lives of 32 people and wound 17 others. Screams pierced the silence. Students began jumping out of windows, hiding in bathrooms, diving under tables and under the bodies of their murdered friends for shelter. One girl, so traumatized by what she had seen, jumped out the window of her classroom and sprinted all the way across campus before collapsing in front of the basketball coliseum. Mass chaos ensued and ended only with the gunman's suicide as he heard the police ramming down the doors.

Jarrett Lane, a promising student, vibrant young man, member of the church I grew up in, and precious son of Tracey Lane, lost his life in the Virginia Tech massacre. His death rocked the sleepy town of Narrows and plunged a community, a nation, into mourning.

As I write this chapter, it's been five years since Jarrett's death. Tracey no longer gets phone calls or flowers on a daily basis, and since that time she's gone back to school, given back to her community and church, and tried to help her family and community heal. She's living proof that there's hope after significant and traumatic loss and is eager to tell the world about God's grace as she walked through this mess. What follows are four ways Tracey believes God provided for her before and during her walk through grief. Consider them her words of wisdom, just for you.

1. Build your foundation now.

As I spoke with Tracey for this chapter, the passage from Luke 6:47-48 came to mind:

> "Everyone who comes to me and hears my words and does them, I will show you what he is like: he is like a man building a house, who dug deep and laid the foundation on the rock. And when a flood arose, the stream broke against that house and could not shake it, because it had been well built."

I think it's important to start with the fact Tracey had built "her house," or life, on the rock before tragedy took her son from her. A life spent in serving the church, time in the Word, consistent growth in her walk with Christ—these were the things that made her foundation secure, so that when the rains came, she was able to come out on the other side of the storm standing.

Her house was well built.

What does that mean? It means that a long time before Jarrett died, Tracey had given her life to Jesus and was pursuing an intimate relationship with him. She had already settled the answers to many of the questions that would assail her during that time of grief, and she was able to cling to the truth of God's Word because she had already seen him prove himself to her over and over again throughout her life.

My guess is that Tracey never thought her years spent pursuing a deep relationship with Christ would be needed to prepare her for losing her son in such a horrific way. But then, isn't that just the point? None of us knows what the day will bring or when the storms will come. We look at our children and dream about what they'll become, but do we entertain the notion that they might not grow up? Might not become who we thought God made them to be? No, at least not for any length of time. It's just too painful to think about our children dying before us. Rightfully so.

And while it isn't a popular thing to say, many of the students and teachers who died that day did so without Christ. Entire families were left to grieve alone, without the hope of heaven. In Tracey's words, "I can't even imagine not having God to carry me through this."

The point? Build your house on the rock of God's Word, the truth of who his Son is, and what he did *now*. Don't wait until tomorrow to get to know the God who loved you enough to send his only Son to die for your sins, and don't be content with just believing the basic tenants of the Christian faith. Build. Here's how:

Step One: If you haven't placed your faith in Jesus as your Savior, do it now. If you need help knowing how to do that, please see page 165.

Step Two: Find a group of local believers (Christians who meet together on a regular basis) and start going. They won't be perfect, but commit to learning more about what it means to walk out the Christian faith with them by your side.

Step Three: Find time every day to pray and get to know God through his Word. Ask God to make the Bible come alive to you, speak to your life situation, and provide the guidance you need to follow after him.

Step Four: Say *yes* to God. Commit to obeying his Word and ask him to give you the strength you need to do it.

These steps don't guarantee protection from the "nonsensicals" of life. Bad things will still happen to you after you become a Christian. In fact, really bad things might happen to you. But you will be prepared because of one, unchanging piece of information:

> A life built on truth withstands the storms.

A life built on truth withstands the storms.

2. Try hard not to walk through life alone.

The reason I described the little town of Narrows in such detail at the beginning of this chapter is because it was the very nature of a small town that played a huge part in Tracey's healing.

Within minutes of hearing about the shootings and piecing together the idea that Tracey's son might not be coming home, Tracey's deacon just showed up on her doorstep. My heart just bursts with pride at the way he and the people of Narrows swooped in and cared for Tracey and her family in real, tangible ways after Jarrett's death.

Everyone wanted to help. Everyone grieved. And in ways as simple as freezable food, beautiful flowers, and even holding her as she found out the news that would change her life, the people of Narrows and its surrounding towns reached out to let her know she wasn't alone.

Many of the students killed that day were from big cities, where neighbors don't know each other as well and church members may not even know each other's names. Parents and siblings were left to deal with their losses alone, unrecognized by their communities and peers. And that just seems so very sad.

I realize not everyone can live in a small town. My husband and I left Narrows over ten years ago ourselves. It's not possible for everyone to have an entire community surround them during tragedy. But it is possible to invest in a sample of your community, regardless of its size.

Are you invested in a church? Have you joined a Sunday school class or small group? Are you investing in the lives of others, living out your life alongside of other people, sharing your journey? If not, start making steps in that direction today. My husband's work schedule makes it very easy for us to be isolated. It requires a substantial amount of effort to make ourselves get up on Sunday morning when he's worked until 3:00 a.m. the night before. It isn't easy for him to stay out late for group activities or time with friends on a Friday night when he has to be up at 5:00 o'clock the next morning. But we do it.

Why?

Because we believe God designed Christians to love, support, and live out life with other Christians.

The fact of the matter is, it doesn't matter if you live in a small town or not. If you choose not to invest in relationships, they won't be there when you need them most. Make a choice today to open your life and heart, and pray that God will bring you friends to do life with.

3. Keep talking to God.

In our interview, I asked Tracey if she ever experienced any anger with God over Jarrett's death. Her reply? "Of course. But he's big enough to handle anything I throw his way.

"When I asked God why he took my son—so full of life, such a bright future—when I was tempted to get mad at God, or walk away from him, I remembered all the days of our lives are written in his book. Not one of us is promised tomorrow. I believe Jarrett's time on this earth was done. He had fulfilled his mission, left his legacy, and I have peace knowing I was the best mother for him I possibly could have been. The gunman at Virginia Tech did not take my son's life. God's plan for him had simply been fulfilled."

God already knows what's in your heart, friend. He knows if you're mad at him, feeling distant, or distrusting of his motives and love. Remember this: Christ died while we were yet sinners (Romans 5:8). That means Jesus willingly endured the shame and brutality of death on the cross knowing you and I were going to sin. In fact, while we were still sinning, entrenched in only caring about our own selfish gain, laughing at him, he pursued us with all the power of heaven. Why? Because of his great love. It's a love like no other, and it's big enough to handle all your emotions and mine.

Tell him how you feel. Confess your emotions, doubts, and deep concerns to him, and allow him to prove his love to you all over again. Just run to his arms. They're big enough to hold you.

4. Refuse to let go of hope.

If there's one thing Tracey really wants other moms who have experienced tragedies, losses, or loss of dreams for their children to know, it's this:

"There is life beyond the tragedy. It's hard to see that or accept it when you're in the middle of your darkest time. There will be days when the pain of your loss will threaten to overcome you, take you away to a place you don't want to go. But one day, you'll wake up and notice the sky is a beautiful shade of blue. You'll see the glory of the clouds and remember how much you loved them. You'll feel the warmth of the sun, laugh at a joke, smile at a stranger, and remember life can be good. When that day comes, hold it in your heart, because you've been given a gift from God. Pass it on. Comfort others with the comfort you've been given and watch what joy that brings to your life."

It took me months to fully recover from my own season of loss, and sometimes I still have sadness hit me out of nowhere. I've learned to take those emotions as they come, allow myself to feel them as deeply as possible, and dig my way out by remembering all of the goodness in my life. I've also realized, as I look back on my own grief process, that Tracey's four steps are what got me through that difficult season, too.

I became a Christian when I was just nine years old, and really started walking closely with the Lord when I was twenty. I had almost ten solid years of significant growth as a Christian before the first tragedy of my life hit. In that time, I recommitted my life to the Lord, studied the Word as much as possible, learned to pray, surrounded myself with godly, stronger friends, and refused to give up fighting for what I believed in (not all at once, and not always very well). Sometimes, I missed the mark. Sometimes, I lost hope and had to fight to find it again. Sometimes, I wanted to wave the white flag and go live on the beach like Jimmy Buffet—blender in hand, blown-out flip flops taking me wherever the wind blew. But I never fully caved to those failures and unrealistic desires. Why? Because God cultivated a deep well of gratitude in me based on his work on the cross. The more I studied it, the more grateful I became. The more grateful I became, the more loyal my heart was to God, trusting his ways above my own—no matter what.

> An eternal perspective can give you hope that there's purpose and provision for every step you take.

Truthfully, Tracey's steps apply to the big things and the little things of life. You don't have to have lost your only son to need the grace of God to keep you going. A simple bad day can make your whole life feel like it's in shambles, and an eternal perspective can give you hope that there's purpose and provision for every step you take.

I've learned it's foolish to rush grief, and that it winds its way through our hearts and minds, affecting layers we didn't know we even had. Sometimes we just have to give ourselves time and admit we're helpless to change by ourselves. Remember, the place of our greatest weakness can unleash the power of God's greatest grace.

I'm *not* saying my child, or Tracey's, died just so we could change, grow, and become more like Jesus. But I *am* saying it would be a waste not to let them make us more like Jesus…

My time with Tracey was such a gift, and I'm so grateful to her for allowing me into this sacred part of her heart. One of the things she said that I don't think I'll ever forget was that she knew Jarrett wouldn't want her life to stop because of his death. She knew from the beginning that this would be the hardest season she would ever walk through, but knowing how much Jarrett loved life, how much he wanted to give and get everything he could from life while he was here, helped her to want to love life again too.

Keep looking up, friend. I know you'll see the sun again soon.

Chapter 10

Moving from Weariness to Worship

Stacey

My grandpa turned ninety on 11/11/11. I can still see the old black-and-white picture my grandma used to keep of him in his Army uniform. Handsome and determined, he carved out a good living for his family in a small town.

His mama, my great-grandma, was a weary mom. He was her baby. And when she was so weary she couldn't take it anymore, she left him with his oldest sister. My great-grandfather was an alcoholic, and truth be told, my great-grandma had had enough of life as mom and raising babies and figuring out how to put one foot in front of the other. So she left. I think of my granddaddy and wonder if he ever asked where his mama went. Could he understand the kind of weary that finds it easier to leave?

My great-grandma is not the only one. As it turns out, more and more mothers are leaving behind life as mom these days.

> While divorce rates have remained stable over the past 30 years, the number of single fathers living with their children has increased from 679,000 in 1982 to 2.23 million in 2011, according to the U.S. Census Bureau. Such men now make up 20% of single parents, up from 10% in 1960.[1]

My great-grandma's blood runs through my heart. I understand. I'm a weary mom too. How do I learn from the legacy of leaving? How do I fight with all I am to love deeper, longer, and harder than she could? Truthfully, I don't want to leave my family physically. I'm guessing you don't either. But what about when I leave emotionally because I'm buried under the weight of it all? Let's be real. We do leave in some ways. Like when we...

- plug in online too much
- eat to cope with stress
- drink alcohol to get through the day
- watch hours of television to get lost in a story

I can honestly say I have done each one of these things to numb the weariness (except when I drink to get through the day it is usually coffee). When we withdraw in these ways for long periods of time, we run the risk of hurting our families as well. Taken too far we might even find ourselves struggling with addictive behaviors.

> In addiction treatment, we talk about the fact that there's a void...Whatever that void may be—whether it's emotional, spiritual, physical—typically, we're trying to fill it.[2]

I believe the answer is laying down the habit of weariness and embracing a heart of worship for the Lord.

The void we feel in our poured out lives as moms is real. Blaise Pascal called it "a God shaped vacuum" and there is only one thing that can fill us up. I believe the answer is laying down the habit of weariness and embracing a heart of worship for the Lord. Because anything less than the very presence of Jesus will never satisfy. The problem for me is lingering in the weariness and letting it take me to other places where fear, defeat, and anger live. I need a remedy that will quickly serve to raise me up. You see, weary lays me low, but worship raises me up. My weariness bows to the one I was made to worship. He really does want to lift us up. He wants to fill us with his presence and turn our dry and weary hearts into gushing rivers of joy. But how do we position our hearts to receive what we need from the Lord?

Worship rolls out the red carpet
for the presence of the Lord.
—PRISCILLA SHIRER[3]

My heart knew it needed to worship. God was, as usual, one step ahead of me and orchestrated a moment of worship for my heart last fall during a church service. I love when he does that. It was as though he made an appointment with only me at the altar in the front of the church to pray. See, I came that particular morning a dried-up well. I was a broken mess of a mom. My husband had been out of town for about a week and I was at the end of myself. We sang all Sunday long until I could not sing anymore. I found my heart being stirred and so I went to spend time bowed low with the One who had whispered, "Come." I confess, I don't go to the altar often. But I knew where he wanted to meet me that morning. And meet me he did.

As soon as my knees hit the carpet, the words began to pour out. Admitting my sins, one by one they rolled out. "I can't do this. I can't do this…I am such a disappointment as a mom. Oh, how I've yelled. I'm so sorry, Lord." I began to cry ugly. He was gentle and loving in his quiet response to me.

I sat at the altar, a heap of tears flowing down, knowing that in his grace he covers everything. Every. Single. Thing. And not once does he disappoint or condemn.

Isaiah 61:3 says that God desires to "give us a garment of praise instead of a faint spirit." This is exactly what He did for me that morning. I left with my weariness laid down and a hope filled heart for the first time in weeks.

We were made for worship and nothing makes the weariness flee more than laying down our smallness and basking in the glory of the One called Holy and True. Do you know the hymn "Turn Your Eyes Upon Jesus?" It has always been my favorite because of this line:

> Turn your eyes upon Jesus, look full in His wonderful face. And the things of earth will grow strangely dim, in the light of His glory and grace.[4]

It is sometimes easier for me to look full in his wonderful face at church while my kids are busy at Sunday school and my pastor has delivered the Word of God on a platter for my heart. Moments like I described above don't happen every Sunday. Most of the time I feel pretty okay while I'm sitting in the pew. I don't know about you, but I need his glory and grace more the other six days of the week when I'm crying in my coffee cup wondering how I'm going to make it through the day. So how do we roll out the red carpet for the presence of the Lord Monday through Saturday? How do we worship God in the small places of our lives and make the most difference in how we live them? Because *really* turning to those other things— food, TV, smartphones—is a form of worship: misplaced, idolatrous worship which does not satisfy our heart's true desire.

Gratitude Leads to Worship

If worship rolls out the red carpet for the presence of the Lord, then gratitude is the thread the carpet is made from. I have learned this lesson over and over again as I have made a gratitude list to purposefully count my blessings. Ann Voskamp says, "It's habits that can imprison you and it's habits that can free you. But when thanks to God becomes a *habit*—so *joy* in God becomes your *life*."[5]

Weariness for me is a habit of my heart. I get bogged down by the things of life because—let's face it—life is hard. I don't want to be imprisoned by my weariness habit anymore. My thanksgiving, my daily counting of joy-filled gifts, unlocks the prison and sets me free.

As I am purposefully grateful for daily gifts all around me, joy fills my heart and I find Jesus right there at the kitchen table, while taking a walk with my girls, or as I tuck them into bed. When I find him, my heart can't help but worship.

Weariness is a habit of the heart.

Some days, the joy gifts bubble up. And some days, it seems, pour gloom. Take last week for instance. It rained. Like a lot. We were stuck indoors for days and my kids were crazy. I found myself dreadfully unmotivated and wondering how in the world I was ever going to get moving. And then I read this verse from 1 Chronicles 16:27. "Splendor and majesty are before him, strength and joy are his dwelling place."

I wonder how long it will take until this truth truly sinks down deep in my heart. I am a dreadfully slow learner. Here I am counting gifts, looking for reasons for joy and really the only one I need is here. The *joy* dwelling place is found in the Lord. Do I want joy to overflow? Do I need strength for unmotivated days? Yes. And Yes. Do you?

It isn't really all that difficult. Let's go to the joy dwelling place and take a good long look at his splendor and majesty. I'm guessing that when we do, even rainy days and Mondays won't get us down. We'll count them, too. And the joy will spread.

Margin Is the Art of Being Still

Being still is absolutely essential to worshipping in our everyday life. If you ask me, this might be the hardest thing for a mother to do. Our lives move dreadfully fast from sunup to sundown. What is margin? I have come to realize it is simply the art of being still. Margin is the whitespace in our life that allows us to slow down, gather ourselves, and fix our eyes on the Lord.

Like art, margin doesn't happen on its own. We have to create it in some way. In fact, we may have to fight for it. Straight up I'm going to tell you this is the one thing I need most to move from weariness to worship. As a mom of four, it is vital to my life. When margin is squeezed out, I am not the woman God wants me to be and I begin to fall back on my fleshly habits of anger, emotional withdrawal, and playing the martyr. You know all about martyrdom, right? "Oh, I'll do it. I'm the ONLY one who does anything around here." Oh friends, that Stacey is not pretty in any way, shape, or form.

There are a few ways I'm creating margin in my life. The first is by getting up about an hour before my family does each morning. I didn't start with an hour. I started years ago with about 15 minutes. I found this time so life-giving I kept adding more minutes. What happens during this time is beautifully illustrated in this verse: "The Spirit of God has made me, and the breath of the Almighty gives me life" (Job 33:4). Each morning I meet with God, he breathes life into my weary heart. It sounds simple, and maybe in some ways it is. Most assuredly, I will tell you, he meets me without fail.

The second way I try to create margin in my life is unplugging from the sometimes noisy world of social media. Sundays, while not a true Sabbath rest for any mother, myself included, is a day I choose for the most part to put down my smartphone and refrain from chatting online. I try to be silent as well as listen more closely to the voice of the Lord. As a writer, blogger, and all-around communicator, I love Twitter, Facebook, and Instagram. But you know what? Nobody needs to hear from me 24/7/365. So I turn it off.

One of my goals for the future is to take one weekend each month for margin. This sounds like a huge undertaking, but I'm motivated to try it anyway. My girls are busy and involved in many activities and with friends. So I don't necessarily see this weekend time as me just sitting in my big red chair reading and sipping tea quietly. Plus, for some reason my family still appreciates eating dinner and having clean clothes. So even though I'd love to sneak away to a cabin by the sea, this time will look a lot more like real life. But what I'd like to see is more white space in these weekends for soul-reviving activities like having coffee with a friend, lingering over a book, or making my family's favorite meal while singing in the kitchen. I want this time to be purposely slower without the rush of doing and producing. If this works even on a semi-monthly basis I think it would yield dividends in my life.

Let Your Heart Sing

One of my all-time favorite books is *Hinds Feet on High Places,* by Hannah Hurnard. The main character is a girl named Much-Afraid (go ahead and insert my name here). In this beautiful allegory, Much-Afraid is invited to go to the high places by the Good Shepherd. She must take a long journey to get there, and along the way she encounters many difficulties. She climbs mountains, walks in the desert, and survives storms. The chapter in the book that has always spoken most clearly to my heart is entitled, "Into the Mist." In it, Much-Afraid was overwhelmed by her situation and could not see a way out. She grew weary by the moment and listened to the voices of Resentment, Bitterness, and Self-Pity. She stumbled about and limped along, directionless. She was completely miserable and on the verge of giving up altogether.

Sound familiar?

Are you trudging along overwhelmed by the daily exhausting, never-ending task of mothering? Do you wonder if you are on the right path and if the way you are taking is in fact getting you anywhere? Have Resentment, Bitterness, and Self-Pity shown up in your home and made themselves permanent houseguests? Have you come to the very end of yourself?

If you just closed your eyes and raised your hand in agreement, sister, I am right there with you. See, this weary mom thing is not something I have lived, learned, and moved on from. It is what I'm living and writing my way through right now. As I put words on paper to hopefully encourage your heart, I'm speaking to my own heart too. I have not arrived. I am a work in progress standing side by side with you.

So what can we do with all this trudging around in the mist of weariness? What did Much-Afraid do?

> At last, one afternoon, when the only word which at all described her progress is to say that she was slithering along the path, all muddy and wet and bedraggled from constant slips, *she decided to sing* (emphasis mine).[6]

The most amazing thing happened as she sang—she cheered a bit. The voices faded away, and to her great surprise she saw the Good Shepherd coming toward her. He was smiling and receiving her song, which really was a sacrifice of praise. She didn't feel like singing, but she did it anyway.

Do you want to know something? I absolutely love to sing. But some days, when I just want to give up, I forget that. I forget the song God himself has written on my heart. Instead I listen to voices all around me that tell me to eat a mini pint of Java Chip ice cream and call my mom to complain. I think I'm alone in my journey and I forget that my Good Shepherd is right there with me the whole time. It seems so simple, but girl, we must find a song to sing on our most weary days. Songs have a powerful way of engaging our hearts even if, unlike me, you don't particularly like to sing out loud. You can speak your song or write it down if you like. But where can we find a song?

I Need Thee Every Hour

I grew up in a tiny Baptist church in small town in Southern Indiana. We had old fashioned hymn sings every Sunday night. The pastor would say, "What song do you want to sing?" And one by one people would holler out their favorites. Luckily, Lois sat at the piano and she knew them all by heart. We'd all sing together the first and last verse and at the end, someone would say, "Amen."

These days, in the contemporary worship service that I attend we don't sing a lot of hymns. But that doesn't stop the Lord from dropping them into my heart from time to time with a sweet memory. One day a while back, I was getting my girls ready for bed and the words to "I Need Thee Every Hour" came to mind:

> I need Thee.
> Oh I need Thee.
> Every hour I need Thee.
> Oh bless me now my Savior,
> I come to thee.

And just like that the words stuck. I sang it all week. It became a prayer of sorts as I went about my days. Like Much-Afraid, my heart was lifted and my eyes turned toward Jesus.

Now this is the point where I get to tell you that sometimes Jesus likes to show off for me. He likes to add an exclamation point in my life when I least expect it. Does he do that for you, too? I'm sure he does. So the story continues with me once again sitting in church the following Sunday. Remember me saying that we don't sing a lot of hymns these days? Remember me telling you that I grew up on them? Well, guess what hymn our worship leader began to play? I am not even kidding you when I say he started playing "I Need Thee Every Hour." I almost fell over right there on the spot. The Good Shepherd slipped into the pew beside me, put his arm around me, and said, "Sweet girl, you must have a song to sing." I cried tears of joy. My heart worshipped.

This whole event left me breathless for Jesus in a way I had not been in quite some time. I became curious about this hymn so I looked it up online. I found out it was written by a girl like me. A housewife in Brooklyn named Annie Hawks wrote it in her kitchen in June 1872. Do you think maybe that she was feeling a little weary and worn as well? Was this the song she was singing in order to better fix her eyes on Jesus? I think that might be the case.

See, the thing about worship is that it acknowledges in the very deepest part of our souls that we need Him. We can't take this journey on our own. We aren't supposed to. Needing him every hour is not defeat. It is an appetite put there by God that only he can fill. Our daily moving toward him through worship is an acknowledgment that we were made for nothing less. We need the very presence of the Lord to strengthen and guide us. We need him every hour. Here is where we find hope.

> Needing him every hour is not defeat. It is an appetite put there by God that only he can fill.

Where are you today? Do you need to spend some time today bowed low with the Grace Giver? Do you need to lay down the weariness and begin to say thank you instead? He wants to meet you. He may have an appointment with you at the altar or maybe he just wants you to sing a song in the kitchen just for him. Either way, he wants to whisper into your heart that he loves you and will never let you go. I promise, when you come to the end of yourself and you choose to worship, your weary heart will sing once more with hope.

Chapter 11

When You Need HOPE Now
Stacey

I loved watching Charlie Brown when I was growing up. Every holiday we were treated to a visit from this motley crew of kids. They taught us about life and relationships in simple comic strip form. My heart broke for Charlie Brown as he tried hard to kick the football, and ended up falling down more times than we could count. You couldn't stay sad for long, because Snoopy would show up and make us smile with his shenanigans. How perfect is that?

Do you know which character made me crazy? No, it isn't Lucy in all her bossiness. I have a whole lot of her in me. The character I'm referring to is Pig Pen. Do you remember him and his perpetual cloud of dust? It seemed to me that he was comfortable with his mess. In fact, everyone else thought so too. Do you realize that no one ever commented about his appearance? Maybe it was because they were accepting him as he was. Kids do that. But maybe it was because they thought, "Why bother?" Or, perhaps they all had a mess they were trying to hide, too. To point out his meant they had to own up to their own.

Help, I'm Turning into Pig Pen

Do you ever wonder why God bothers with us? Wouldn't it just be easier if he looked the other way or shoved us in his heavenly junk drawer and saved our sorting out for a rainy day? Or better yet, why doesn't he use someone who has it together far more than we do? There is always someone prettier, skinnier, and more together than me. Surely, that mom is available. She probably even has an app on her phone that keeps her mess in check.

Not me. I think if it is possible I've grown in my messiness over the years. I remember as a kid being mortified if one Barbie shoe was out of place. I only turned in neat papers and I always went above and beyond the call. But lately, I can't get my mess together. Oh, at times I still act like I have it all together, like Lucy. But I feel more and more like Pig Pen. The mess swirling around me this week looks like a disastrous start to potty training my fourth daughter, too much fast food for my family, and a pending war in my living room between my dishes and laundry if I don't start peace talks soon.

What is worse than all of this is the mess that has taken up residence in my heart. It is big I tell you. I don't like who or what has moved into this space. I can't even imagine why God in all his glory would choose to reside there for more than ten seconds.

Oh but for grace! His great big huge *How Great Thou Art* grace pours over me the moment I feel like I am a lost cause and he reminds me who he is. A brief look into the Gospel of Luke tells me...

- he came to a messy world
- he was born in a stable
- his parents, pretty much unmarried
- their lives were far from perfect
- he chose to walk with messy people
- his best friends, fishermen
- he was known to hang out with tax collectors
- he left his ministry in the hands of uneducated men

- he ministered to even messier people
- he ate with sinners
- he let a scandalous woman wash his feet
- he rubbed elbows with the rejects of society

And truthfully, he didn't get along too well with all the good and safe people. The "Lucy" types who had it all together didn't really need him. Time and time again Jesus met people in their mess and offered them hope. And they were never the same.

This same Jesus wants to meet us in the middle of our mess, too. He wants to do a work in us and then through us. He isn't going to settle for just cleaning up our circumstances. We know he can do that in a heartbeat and sometimes he does. I like how the Message version of the Bible affirms this in Ephesians 3:20-21:

> God can do anything, you know—far more than you could ever imagine or guess or request in your wildest dreams! He does it not by pushing us around but by working within us, his Spirit deeply and gently within us.

Did you catch that? His plan is to do far more than we can imagine. He does it by working within us. He wants to teach us about his character and reveal his heart for us. He wants to whisper in our ears, *Hope is here.* And in the process he changes more than our mess—he changes us. What a glorious promise that is for our hearts today!

Today Is the Day for HOPE

Today is a great day to take one step toward hope and one giant leap out of weariness. We can do it together and trust hope is here. I love this precious reminder from Matthew 12:21 about Jesus. It says, "And His name will be the hope of all the world" (NLT). Did you know his name actually is Hope? It all comes back to our relationship with the One whose name holds precisely what our weary hearts need. A while back, God gave us an acronym using the word

HOPE. We love to use it to share this message more easily. Plus, let's face it, as moms we have so many things to remember any time we can keep it easy it is a win-win for everyone.

H: Honestly admit where you are.

O: Openly invite Christ into your mess.

P: Pray continually.

E: Encourage your heart with God's Word.

Honestly admit where you are.

Girls, get your white flags out. It is time to take off the veil of *fine* and be honest about what is going on in your heart and homes. I think we all struggle to do this. Every mom. Every woman. We feel the need to keep smiling and the truth is, we are dying under the weight of it all.

When I finally admitted I was fresh out of amazing, God leaned in and whispered, "I'm so glad you said something. I've been waiting for you." He knew all along. But I needed to tell the truth about my situation before it would begin to change. When I admitted the mess in my heart, it was as though the light of hope switched on for me.

There is so much freedom in being honest. Secrets keep a power over us and paralyze us in dark places. The first step is to speak it to yourself and then tell your husband or a trusted friend. They need to know, too. You may think they will judge you, but I'm guessing they already know something isn't quite right. Weariness wants to keep you alone and in the dark. Don't stay there. Be honest and move forward.

Openly invite Christ into your mess.

While God is super willing to join us in our mess, he appreciates an invitation as well. I like to describe him as the perfect gentleman. He won't force his way into any part of your life you haven't asked him to come into. I love this reminder from Isaiah 41:10: "Fear not, for I am with you; be not dismayed, for I am your God; I will strengthen you, I will help you, I will uphold you with my righteous right hand." He is waiting to help us. He longs to strengthen us as moms. He wants to hold us up with his powerful hand. We need him to do that today.

If you are ready for God to meet you right where you are and do more than you can imagine, would you join us in the following prayer?

> *Lord, today I want to honestly admit where I am. I am tired beyond the normal. I am a weary mom who needs a fresh encounter with you. Please work in my messy heart. Make it a place where you love to reside. Fill it with your presence and begin working on the inside who you want me to be on the outside. I believe you want to do more than I can possibly imagine. I invite you to start right now. I know it will not happen overnight. I might take two steps forward and two steps back. Thank you for walking with me, Jesus, and being patient with me. Thank you for making me a mom in the first place. My prayer is that my family will be the first to see Hope at work in me. Amen.*

Pray continually.

Prayer is a place where we pour out our hearts and pause to hear God's voice. Having invited him into our mess, we need to continue this life-giving conversation on a daily basis. Through prayer we can ask him to supply our greatest needs and fight our biggest battles.

David was one who understood the conversation of prayer. He was always crying out and God was always lifting him up. I think this is beautifully illustrated in Psalm 61:1-4:

> Hear my cry, O God, listen to my prayer; from the end
> of the earth I call to you when my heart is faint. Lead me
> to the rock that is higher than I, for you have been my

refuge, a strong tower against the enemy. Let me dwell in your tent forever! Let me take refuge under the shelter of your wings.

David poured out his heart and then something beautiful happens just after verse 4. He paused. Some translations of Scripture use the word *Selah,* which is a musical term meaning "to pause" or "be silent." What was David doing during the pause? He was reflecting and listening. The next few words show us what God spoke to David in the middle of this holy pause: "For you have heard my vows; you have given me the heritage of those who fear your name" (Psalm 61:5).

David knew God had heard him as he poured out his heart. He paused and God spoke to him the very word of encouragement he needed. As a result David's heart overflowed with praise. "I will never stop singing your praise; as long as I live, I will fulfill my promise" (Psalm 61:8 The Voice).

Prayer is absolutely vital to connecting us to our source of hope. Sometimes when we are weary we simply forget to talk to Jesus about it. Instead we settle for steadily complaining to others, looking to gain their sympathy. What we need is a refuge and a strong tower of hope. With a simple prayer we can cry out to God and find both.

Encourage your heart with God's Word.

Do you know one of the reasons God's Word exists is to stir up your hope? Romans 15:4 tells us this very thing: "For whatever was written in former days was written for our instruction, that through endurance and through the encouragement of the Scriptures we might have hope."

God gave us Scripture to encourage us and give us hope because he knew we'd need to see it in black and white. He knew we would need to hold his words in our hands so we could get them in our hearts. But God in his goodness doesn't just stop there. He wants us to be filled abundantly with hope:

> May the God of hope fill you with all joy and peace in believing that through the power of the Holy Spirit you may abound in hope (Romans 15:13).

God is our source of hope. He himself wants to fill you not just with hope, but with joy and peace as well. As we encounter him in the pages of the Bible, our faith grows. Through the power of the Holy Spirit, he ignites our hope and it overflows exceedingly.

Does that make you want to stand on your chair right now and cheer? It does me. I love God's Word. I know life is crazy busy times a million for you, friend. It is for me, too. But the one place you can be assured of meeting the God of Hope on a daily basis is in the pages of his Word. He dwells there. Making time to read it, meditate on it, and memorize hope-filled truth will make a significant difference in your life.

There is no magic wand I can wave over you to encourage your heart with God's Word instantly. You simply have to dive in yourself. You have to make time for it.

When I was a little girl I wanted to jump off the high dive at our city pool. I was terrified and more than once went halfway up the ladder and came straight back down. I could not bring myself to take the leap of faith.

Halfway through the summer, during the Fourth of July festivities, my whole family went swimming at the pool. My dad was a great swimmer and he loved diving. I happened to mention to him I wanted to go off the high dive but I was scared. He said, "Well, I'll come with you. I'll get in the water and I'll be here when you dive in. I'll make sure you are okay."

Guess what I did? I climbed up. I walked to the edge of the board. And now, with my daddy swimming in the deep end, I jumped. He was by my side immediately before my head came up for air. Having him in the pool made all the difference.

Friend, I promise you this with all my heart: When you dive into God's Word, Jesus himself will be waiting for you and your heart will be encouraged.

Hope Is the Gospel

Do you want to know the truth? Hope is really the gospel. We all must come to a place where we realize we can't, but he can. We can cry out to him to meet us in our mess and be real to us in our lives right now. His Word strengthens and guides us. Since Jesus is the word made flesh, according to John 1:1, what we are saying is "Lord, be strong in our lives."

I preach this HOPE to myself over and over every single day. I need the reminder because I am the needy one, too. I cling to it. This gospel of HOPE is my answer.

> The gospel is so foolish (according to my natural wisdom) so scandalous (according to my conscience) and so incredible (according to my timid heart) that it is a daily battle to believe the full scope of it as I should. There is simply no other way to compete with the forebodings of my conscience, the condemning of my heart, and the lies of the world with the devil than to overwhelm such things with daily rehearsing of the gospel.[1]

The gospel is hope. It is for your heart and mine. The reason it resonates in our hearts is because Jesus is the one doing the talking. He wants to overwhelm us with truth and silence our condemning hearts. He wants to stir up our hope all day long. So let's preach on, Mama. Let's preach on.

Our Prayer of Blessing

As we close the pages of this book we want you to know we are not closing our story. Brooke and I want to get one thing straight:

We are not experts. We're just weary moms. We will never tell you how to organize your home, discipline your kids, or streamline your budgets. These are good and worthy things that may make your lives easier, but this is not what "Hope" is about.

Our stories are still very much being written. We are two moms who met each other and God in the middle of our messy lives. This book is our honest cry. His hands are still working on these lumps of clay. The words we have written on the pages of this book matter to us because we are clinging to the truth behind them each and every day. We are grateful God sees the beautiful lovely inside our hearts and calls us his own.

We would love to pray a prayer of blessing over you from the book of Psalms. It is our heart's desire that all you see in this book is Hope coming for you.

> May the Eternal's answer find you, come to rescue you when you desperately cling to the end of your rope. May the name of the True God of Jacob be your shelter. May He extend *hope and* help to you from His *holy* sanctuary and support you from *His sacred city of* Zion. May He remember all that you have offered Him; may your burnt sacrifices serve as a prelude to His mercy.
>
> [pause]
>
> May He grant the dreams of your heart and see your plans through to the end (Psalm 20:1-4 The Voice).

When you cling to the end of your rope, we pray you see him. He is your shelter. He will support you. He is the answer.

He is Hope for the Weary Mom.

Q&A with Stacey and Brooke

We asked you to share some of the burning questions on your mind about the authors behind *Hope for the Weary Mom*. Nothing was off-limits! We picked our favorites and are thrilled to be sharing a little bit of our behind-the-scenes with you, friend!

1. How did you come to Christ?

Stacey I don't remember not going to church. As a child I grew up knowing that "Jesus loves me for the Bible tells me so." This is mostly because my mom rededicated her life to Christ right before I was born. She was faithful to not only take me to church but also demonstrate to me a life of faith built on prayer and the study of God's Word. I accepted Christ at age nine when I read a book my pastor gave me on how to become a Christian. Shortly after that, I was baptized.

It wasn't until I was a student at Indiana University that my rooted faith began to grow. I became involved with a Christian student group called Campus Crusade for Christ and learned what it meant to walk with Christ in the daily aspects of life, share his love with others, and study God's Word with focused determination. I went on mission trips, led small groups, and found a passion to serve God with my whole life.

Brooke I was raised in a sweet little Southern Baptist church in southwestern Virginia. My Sundays were filled with sound biblical teaching and adults who loved me. I was saved and baptized when I was just nine years old, but didn't really start walking closely with the Lord until right before my husband and I started dating in 1999. Ironically, just before we got together, my husband and I had both decided that doing things our way wasn't working, and we entered our relationship committed to doing things God's way from the very beginning.

2. How did you meet your husband?

Stacey My husband, Mike, and I met on a Campus Crusade for Christ Mission Project in Ocean City, New Jersey, in the summer of 1991. He was a student at Miami of Ohio (though later transferred to Ohio University) and I was attending Indiana University. We both knew from the beginning that this was "the one." We dated long distance for two years before e-mail and cell phones existed. (Can you imagine?) He was a true gentleman and paid for my phone bills! We married in April 1994 on a beautiful spring day.

Brooke I've had a crush on my husband since the third grade. Corny, I know, but it's true. When I was an awkward little girl in grade school, this family of all boys moved to our small town and started attending our church. The three brothers, all pretty handsome, were all the rage for quite some time, but my heart belonged to the youngest.

Like all the other girls, I giggled when he walked by, asked him if he would be my boyfriend (he said no), and bought a copy of the school picture he was selling. For just 50 cents I had a picture of the guy for me, nerdy glasses and all.

In the eighth grade, I asked him to go to a dance with me. Well, to be more correct, I had my best friend Jennifer call him and ask if he would go with me to the dance. He said no (again!).

After several hits, misses, and almosts throughout the years, his family began scheming to get us together. I was spending a good deal of time walking with his sister-in-law, Susan, and often, after a hard walk, she would invite me in for lemonade, a movie, or just to chat. Miraculously, he would show up needing to use their weight room or talk to his big brother about something or just work on his truck. We started spending a lot of time together because of our mutual relationships with his brother and sister-in-law, but I was dating someone else and wasn't sure I wanted to throw that relationship away.

One day, after yet another walk with Susan, he offered to drive me home. Now my parents lived just up the street, and he and I both knew I didn't really need to be driven home. I tried to tell him no (honestly, I did!) but he was insistent, so I climbed up in the truck, watched his brother and sister-in-law wave at us, and let him drive me home.

When we got there (30 seconds later) he turned the truck off, looked into my eyes, and told me I was the girl for him…the one he'd been looking for all of his life but didn't know was right in front of him. He respectfully acknowledged I was dating someone else but asked for a chance to prove himself to me.

We started dating about two months later, and he's been the love of my life ever since.

3. What's the biggest bit of parenting advice you whole-heartedly believe in but have trouble practicing?

Stacey This is such a great question. The one that comes to mind currently is "Life is not an emergency," from Ann Voskamp. I'm not sure it is really parenting advice but in my home this is a real issue. As you know, we have four girls. Everything in my home seems to be an emergency. Lost shoes? Emergency! Where is the remote? Emergency! She is looking cross-eyed at me? Emergency! I try very hard to live above the drama, but I am not always successful. I'm praying

God will help me stay calm and not contribute to the emotion. The trouble is, as a one-of-a-kind family, we tend to feed off each other. I know getting enough rest and finding times to just be quiet during my day helps me maintain calm. I am taking baby steps in this area. I wonder if other girl households can relate!

Brooke Don't yell at your kids. Ouch! It hurts to admit that, but it's true. I try SO hard not to yell at my boys, but sometimes I feel like if I don't yell, they'll never hear me over all of the boy noise. Our home is loud most of the time, and our youngest son is just naturally a loud kid. I often find myself raising my voice just to be heard! I lose my cool with them a lot more than I care to admit, but I am getting better at it every day, and I try hard to tell them (and show them) I love them twice as much as I lose it with them.

4. As weary moms (and women in general), how do we encourage each other to quit pretending that everything is okay and just get real with each other?

Stacey I think we have to be willing to tell our own stories. I love that this book is giving some weary moms permission to do so. There is true power in sharing our hearts with other women. Because when we do that, we have the chance to connect on a real level. We can spur one another on and we can pray for each other. As I look back on this past year and the journey with *Hope for the Weary Mom* I am amazed at how many moms thought they were alone. I love that we all know now that we are not.

The truth is, the parts of our stories that are not so bright and shiny are what people most want to hear about. It helps them know they are normal. I think we hide because the enemy has convinced us no one will understand and everyone will think we are crazy. This simply is not the case. We need to tell what is really going on. We can share our story and in the process pass hope on to another mom.

Brooke I love this question! I come from a very private family who likes to keep their "business" (you really have to say that with a Southern accent to get the full effect) to themselves. I get asked a lot about why I share my junk openly, and my answer is always the same:

(a) I want to know if I'm normal or not and (b) so that in the rare event that I actually do something right, another mom might benefit.

Seriously though, I think we all need to quit pretending that the last 50 years of women's lib haven't affected how we think about ourselves. I'm grateful for the opportunity to vote and share my opinions as much as the next woman, but in spite of everything freedom for women got right, I think we also got some things wrong. After years of being told that we can have it all, we feel guilty, or like there's something wrong with us, if we're not doing a good job of being a mom, employee, sister in Christ, sister, daughter, etc., etc...So we don't talk about our failings and disappointments. I've found that by laying my mess out for all the world to see, other women have been freed up to do the same. And the effects are far-reaching! When we admit our weaknesses, we give God permission to be strong for us (but I've already written about that)!

The best way you can encourage other moms to get real about their messes is by getting real about yours. Gently and humbly come alongside one or two moms to start with, and watch what God does as you let it all out.

I won't pretend this "laying it all out there" mentality doesn't come with a bit of fear and trepidation. I often worry that others will judge me too harshly, or worse, judge my children too harshly, placing higher expectations on them than they can handle just because Mama writes. But I've found over time that I just have to release that to the Lord, because walking in obedience to him during this season of my life means sharing my truth. Moms desperately need to know they're not alone, so I trust him to take care of the details.

5. How do you manage your family and your writing schedule?

Stacey We are a busy family of six and managing life at times seems to be a farfetched dream. But there is a lot of truth in the saying that you make time for what is important. When I need to write because something is due, I write. When I need to write because I have a word I need to get out of my head and heart, I write. I can fit it in when I need to.

On a daily basis my day looks like this: I wake up at 6:15 and have my time with Jesus. Sometimes, my response to him is through the written word. After the girls get up, we eat, watch *I Love Lucy*, and start our homeschool day. I'm usually busy teaching, fixing lunch, and doing chores until early afternoon. Most days I write in the afternoon while my girls are playing together. The rest of our day is filled with ballet, daily grocery store errands, and dinner prep. By evening my brain is mush and you would not want to read what I write! On the weekends, I try to write on Saturday morning or Sunday afternoon. My favorite place to write is at Barnes and Noble while eating a vanilla cupcake and drinking a hazelnut latte. Sadly, this happens only once in a blue moon.

Brooke I'm not sure I'm the best person to talk about this, because I'm constantly changing how I approach it. Truthfully, in the beginning of my career I did a really poor job of it, neglecting my family so I could build what I thought was an important following. I wrote a short, inexpensive ebook about all the Lord taught me from that time called *Notes to Aspiring Writers: Your Dream, God's Plan* that really sums up my feelings about a writer's priorities. That being said, with two active, homeschooled young boys and a husband who works shift work, I have to get creative. Since the boys are young, I write most of the time when they're having quiet time or are asleep. For me that means about two hours mid-day and another two after they've gone to bed. If I'm in a serious season of writing (such as for this book) we hire a babysitter one day a week and I try to get up one to two hours earlier in the morning to work. It isn't perfect, but it works for us right now.

6. What are your top three reads for believing moms?

Stacey *Jesus Calling* by Sarah Young. I love this devotional because it is written from the perspective of Jesus to the reader. I find this a perfect daily read when life is at its craziest. I also love the Scriptures listed at the end of each daily reading. I found out recently that this is now an app for your phone. So you can have it with you wherever you go!

Ministry of Motherhood by Sally Clarkson. This was the first book I read that helped me to see my mothering as a discipleship ministry. I realized Jesus understood my life as a mom and his training of the twelve looked a lot like my daily training and molding my girls.

Pursuit of God by A.W. Tozer. This is not a mom book exactly. But I think we need to remember who we are as women of God first. The language in this book is a bit elevated and many times I have to reread the sentences a couple of times. But it sinks soul-deep quickly and will encourage you greatly. I went through this with a group of moms a couple years ago, and though at first they were skeptical, it became their favorite book. This book is one I have read again and again.

Brooke *One Thousand Gifts: A Dare to Live Fully Right Where You Are*, by Ann Voskamp. This book is poetry, but it's so much more than that. In the day-to-day weariness of mothering, we keep the flame of hope going by choosing to be thankful for the good things in our lives. This book will teach you how to do that. It's just beautiful.

Give Them Grace: Dazzling Your Kids with the Love of Jesus, by Elyse Fitzpatrick. This book doesn't offer a cheesy "let your kids get away with everything" kind of grace. It's a deep, challenging, convicting look at how the grace of God changes everything, including how we parent our kids.

A Praying Life: Connecting with God in a Distracting World, by Paul Miller. A true, honest, and gritty look at prayer. While it's not really a parenting book, the author talks a lot about how we do our best parenting on our knees, and I wholeheartedly agree.

Verses for the Weary Mom

2 Corinthians 12:9

But he said to me, "My grace is sufficient for you, for my power is made perfect in weakness." Therefore I will boast all the more gladly of my weaknesses, so that the power of Christ may rest upon me.

John 16:28

I have said these things to you, that in me you may have peace. In the world you will have tribulation. But take heart; I have overcome the world.

Isaiah 41:10

Fear not, for I am with you; be not dismayed, for I am your God; I will strengthen you, I will help you, I will uphold you with my righteous right hand.

Philippians 4:13

I can do all things through Him who strengthens me.

Galatians 6:9

And let us not grow weary of doing good, for in due season we will reap, if we do not give up.

Psalm 121:1–4

I lift up my eyes to the hills. From where does my help come? My help comes from the LORD, who made heaven and earth. He will not let your foot be moved; he who keeps you will not slumber. Behold, he who keeps Israel will neither slumber nor sleep.

Psalm 103:2-5

Bless the LORD, O my soul, and forget not all his benefits, who forgives all your iniquity, who heals all your diseases, who redeems your life from the pit, who crowns you with steadfast love and mercy, who satisfies you with good so that your youth is renewed like the eagle's.

Matthew 11:29-30

Take my yoke upon you, and learn from me, for I am gentle and lowly in heart, and you will find rest for your souls. For my yoke is easy, and my burden is light.

Hebrews 13:20-21

Now may the God of peace who brought again from the dead our Lord Jesus, the great shepherd of the sheep, by the blood of the eternal covenant, equip you with everything good that you may do his will, working in us that which is pleasing in his sight, through Jesus Christ, to whom be glory forever and ever. Amen.

Psalm 116:2 (NLT)

Because he bends down to listen, I will pray as long as I have breath!

Psalm 31:1-5

In you, O LORD, do I take refuge; let me never be put to shame; in your righteousness deliver me! Incline your ear to me; rescue me speedily! Be a rock of refuge for me, a strong fortress to save me! For you are my rock and my fortress; and for your name's sake you lead me and guide me; you take me out of the net they have hidden for me, for you are my refuge. Into your hand I commit my spirit; you have redeemed me, O Lord, faithful God.

Psalm 91:1-2

He who dwells in the shelter of the Most High will abide in the shadow of the Almighty. I will say to the Lord, "My refuge and my fortress, my God, in whom I trust."

Psalm 55:22

Cast your burden on the Lord, and he will sustain you; he will never permit the righteous to be moved.

2 Timothy 1:7

God gave us a spirit not of fear but of power and love and self-control.

John 14:27

Peace I leave with you; my peace I give to you. Not as the world gives do I give to you. Let not your hearts be troubled, neither let them be afraid.

John 3:30

He must increase, but I must decrease.

James 4:8

Draw near to God, and he will draw near to you.

Jeremiah 29:11

For I know the plans I have for you, declares the Lord, plans for welfare and not for evil, to give you a future and a hope.

The Weary Mom Manifesto

I believe God's plans for me are good. Therefore, I commit today that I will never give up on my family, and I will never give up on God's ability to move in their hearts. With his help, I will take the next step of faith even when I feel I can't, because he is the God of miracles.

Name: _____

Witness: _____

Date:_____

Gospel Truths for Weary Moms

We've been loved into repentance by Jesus. He loved us while we were drowning in our sin. He sees us, loves us, and promises to redeem our hurts if we'll open ourselves to him (John 3:16).

Each of us has sinned and messed up. There is no perfect mom out there, and if there's one who says she is, she's lying. When you look at other moms, other women, choose to believe that they're more like you than they are different. We don't have to measure up. Refuse to allow the voice of the enemy (who only wants to kill, steal, and destroy you) to be the loudest voice you hear. Fill your head and heart with the Word. Let God's voice be the one you nurture. He has come to give you abundant life (Romans 3:23, John 10:10).

Acknowledge your need of Christ and invite him to be part of your life. He is knocking at the door of your heart and wants to be part of your life—even the messy parts. Parenting is not a solo act. Just as it takes the Creator God to breathe life into our wombs, it takes the Redeemer God to turn hearts of stone to hearts of flesh (Revelation 3:20, Ezekiel 36:26).

Grow in your relationship with Jesus every day. Set aside regular time to renew your strength from the Lord. Meditate on his Word and allow the truth of it to change the way you act, the way you believe. Choose to believe that it's true and walk out obedience to it every day. If you need practical help doing that, visit Stacey's blog or Brooke's blog. We both talk regularly about living out faith (Romans 12:1-2, Colossians 3:16-17).

Choose to love him and follow him no matter what. Expect hard times, and choose this day whom you will serve. When things don't go the way you want them to, cling all the more tightly to the God who never changes, the same one who gave up his Son so you could find forgiveness from sin (Joshua 24:15, Hebrews 12:1-2,13:8).

If you don't have a local church already, find one. We need other Christians to walk with and live in community beside as we grow to be more like Jesus. They need us, too. We were never meant to be alone (1 Corinthians 12:27, Hebrews 10:24-25).

Kitchen Table Talks
Small Group Ideas with Study Guide

We saw a beautiful picture of weary moms walking together a while back in Austin, Texas. They arrived in groups of two or three with diapers bags and kids in tow. A few moms walked in alone and anxiously scouted out a place to sit at one of the seven tables that filled the room. Each of the seven tables was decorated with flowers and chocolate in the most thoughtful way. Scattered around the room were several women waiting with open hearts and arms ready to hug. Mamas let out heavy sighs of release as kids were safely tucked in the age-appropriate classes. Food was served buffet style alongside a steamy hot cup of coffee. Everyone settled in their seats ready for the first *Kitchen Table Talk* to begin. All eyes looked to Brooke and then to me, and I (Stacey) whispered a prayer: *Lord, only you can fill their hearts. Speak through us. Use our stories and words. Bring Hope to these women today.*

As we began to share, the women eased a bit into their seats. Some took notes. Others dotted their eyes with the tissues sweetly provided on the tables. God honored his Word once again: "For where two or three are gathered in my name, there am I among them" (Matthew 18:20). He came to us like rain and watered the dry places. He moved in and through our hearts and did exactly what he promised he would. His very presence reminded us we were not alone, and the filled-up tables testified that we have sisters who we can walk with in the weary days that motherhood sometimes brings.

The neatest thing happened in Austin toward the end of our first Kitchen Table Talk. We gave the women time to share their hearts and talk through some discussion questions at their tables. What began as a hushed chat turned into a lively discussion among friends. They talked long. They laughed together and bonded over the similarities of their stories. Hearts connected. In fact, we had to interrupt them to conclude our time together. Weary moms joined hands and began to walk together. They clumped and it was a beautiful thing.

We wanted to give you the tools as well to host your own Kitchen Table Talk featuring *Hope for the Weary Mom*. You can use the following study guide to meet weekly or take a morning like we did to feature specific parts of the book. Whatever you decide, we pray you find this guide useful.

Tips for Creating a Meaningful and Well-Organized Study

1. As soon as you decide to lead a group study of *Hope for the Weary Mom*, begin to pray for your members. Ask the Lord to bring the right ones to the group and to be preparing their hearts for what he wants to accomplish in them. Continue to pray for them throughout your time together.

2. Begin and end on time, assuming that time is valuable for each member of your group. Let them know at the first meeting that you aspire to doing this.

3. Consider beginning and ending in prayer, and always ask for prayer requests from the group. However, you might consider putting a system in place to help control the amount of time spent on prayer requests. For example, perhaps you could have each of the women in your group come to class with their request for the week

already written on an index card. Have the members switch cards, pray over them out loud, and commit to praying for the member whose card they have all week.

4. Make sure each woman has a copy of *Hope for the Weary Mom* which is available through your favorite book retailer. If a woman in your group needs financial assistance with the book, seek help from your church to assist her.

5. Decide in advance how you will handle difficult situations that arise within the group. If you need help knowing how to handle conflict, talk to your pastor before the group starts and ask him how he would like you to handle it. Always remember to follow the guidelines of Matthew 18 when dealing with conflict.

6. Feel free to use the wealth of material at the *Hope for the Weary Mom* blog to supplement your reading throughout the study, and connect with other moms leading a study or just reading the book at the Hope for the Weary Mom Facebook page.

7. Make sure you supply tissues for each session.

8. Decide beforehand if you will supply snacks, or if you would like each group member to take turns bringing something for the session.

9. Make a phone number list, and make sure everyone in the group has a way to contact you.

10. For each chapter, you'll find the following helps: Focus Verse, Ice Breaker, Questions for Small Group Discussion, and Action Point. These are here to guide you, but please feel free to add or subtract as you see fit.

11. Have fun!

Chapter 1:

When Your Weakness Is All You Can See

Focus Verses: "But he said to me, 'My grace is sufficient for you, for my power is made perfect in weakness.' Therefore I will boast all the more gladly of my weaknesses, so that the power of Christ may rest upon me. For the sake of Christ, then, I am content with weaknesses, insults, hardships, persecutions, and calamities. For when I am weak, then I am strong" (2 Corinthians 12:9-10).

Ice Breaker: Do you have any funny stories about times when you were at the end of your rope with motherhood? Share them with the group and have a good laugh together.

Questions for Small Group Discussion

1. Where do you usually turn for relief? Can you relate to the story Brooke shared in this chapter of feeling completely overwhelmed?

2. Have you gotten to the place of total breakdown? What did it look like for you?

3. What's one weakness that consistently makes you feel not good enough? What are the things you catch yourself saying about yourself because of this weakness (internal self-talk)?

4. How hard is it for you to hear the voice of God in your daily life?

5. Did you take the "weary mom manifesto" challenge? If so, tell a friend.

Action Point: Commit in prayer today to give your weak areas to God. Then ask him to make himself look good in you because of them.

Chapter 2:
When You're Caught in What You're Not

Focus Verses: "For we are his workmanship, created in Christ Jesus for good works, which God prepared beforehand, that we should walk in them" (Ephesians 2:9-11).

Ice Breaker: Find a short personality test that describes whether you're an introvert or extrovert. Talk about the results as a small group.

Questions for Small Group Discussion

1. Think back to the time before you had kids. What were some of the dreams you had for your life?

2. When was the last time you focused on developing your strengths?

3. How often do you find yourself comparing your strengths to another mom and wishing you had more of hers?

4. Which personality type best fits you? Describe some of the ways the character traits associated with these personality types affect you as a person.

5. Think about 1 Corinthians 12:14, 17-21. What role do you serve in the body of Christ? What can you do to develop that and allow God to use you more fully in this area?

Action Point: At the end of the chapter, Brooke tells you to find a way to get yourself filled. Part of this happens as we learn more about who we are and how God made us. But most of it happens as we trust God enough to let him fill our gaps. What's one way you can actively trust God to take care of your weak spots today?

Chapter 3:
Confronting Carol

Focus Verse: "Come to me, all of you who are weary and carry heavy burdens, and I will give you rest" (Matthew 11:28 NLT).

Ice Breaker: Describe the TV mom you most aspire to be (or maybe flopped at becoming).

Questions for Small Group Discussion

1. Do you have areas of your life where you constantly struggle? Maybe your dishes are piled sky high or your laundry looks like a small mountain. When you look at those visible signs of struggle, what are the first words that pop into your head?

2. Are the words you thought of actually true? If God were telling you how to feel about yourself based on those areas of struggle, would his voice be the same as the one you hear in your mind?

3. How often do you catch yourself comparing your home, job, income, or parenting to someone else's?

4. We have listed verses of hope for the weary mom in the back of this book. Next time you're tempted to think you're all alone in your mess, or that everyone else is doing a better job at this parenting gig than you, sit down, close the door, and let the truth of God's Word wash over you.

5. Are you willing to let others be drawn into your story?

Action Point: Create your own verses of hope and put them in a place where you can see them every day. Share it with another mom and begin to build your clump today by looking up and not sizing up.

Chapter 4:
The Marathon of Mothering

Focus Verse: "The Lord will fight for you, and you have only to be silent" (Exodus 14:14).

Ice Breaker: What is your favorite campout food? Share the recipe or better yet bring some to Bible Study!

Questions for Small Group Discussion

1. If you have younger kids or older kids share what is the hardest part of mothering at this particular age.

2. How have you changed or matured since you became a mother?

3. God's Word has been written to give us hope and instruct us for living. Share one verse you cling to that stirs up hope in your heart.

4. Are you in a place where you need to "break camp" and move forward? What is one step you can take today to do that with faith?

Action Point: Runners often keep a diary about each of their runs and how it went. This week, write a journal about how you ran as a mom. Specifically look for glimpses of God's plan, pace, and provision for you.

Chapter 5:

Redeeming Mommy Guilt

Focus Verse: "For by grace you have been saved through faith. And this is not of your own doing; it is a gift of God, not a result of works, so that no one may boast" (Ephesians 2:8-9).

Ice Breaker: Name one thing you tried to make your mom feel guilty about when you were a child. Did she ever forget to pick you up from school? Were you the only kid who did not eat TV dinners or had really boring stuff in her lunch to trade?

Questions for Small Group Discussion

1. What causes mommy guilt in your life? How is it adding to your weariness?

2. When rooting out the lies we believe it is important to identify the first lie we are prone to accept. Mine is, "God doesn't know what is happening in my life. Therefore I have to take matters into my own hands." You can imagine how much trouble this makes in my life. Would you be brave today and share the first lie you are prone to believe?

3. Which of the grace-filled truths in the "Reclaiming Your Freedom" section speaks most directly to your heart? Why?

4. I believe this is a huge area many moms (myself included) struggle with. How can we pray for you to experience God's freedom in an area you are experiencing mommy guilt?

Action Point: Let's build other moms up instead of tearing them down as demonstrated in this chapter. Find one mom you can encourage with the truth from this chapter and remind her "Guilt has no place in the space of grace."

Chapter 6:
When Gentle Words Won't Come

Focus Verses: "But I have trusted in your steadfast love; my heart shall rejoice in your salvation. I will sing to the Lord, because he has dealt bountifully with me" (Psalm 13:5-6).

Ice Breaker: Choose three people to act out a small demonstration. Have two stand in one corner pretending to have a conversation. Give one of the two a paper cup filled with water. Have the third person walk toward the other two like she's going to join the conversation, but trip at the last second, knocking the cup of water out of the other person's hand.

After cleaning up the mess, have the group leader discuss why the water spilled on the floor. Was it because person number three was clumsy and knocked it to the ground? Or was it because there was water in the cup to begin with? If there'd been no water in the cup, there would've been no water on the floor. Have the group leader discuss how this represents the "what's in the heart comes out" principle.

Questions for Small Group Discussion

1. Are there certain things your children do that cause an immediate physical and emotional reaction to occur in you?

2. Have you ever punished your child for something that was really more *your* issue than his?

3. Do you ever wish God would just snap his fingers and make all your sin (and your children's sin) go away?

4. Why do you think God doesn't do this more often?

5. Have you ever considered that your circumstances aren't

what cause you to lose your gentle words, but what's
already in your heart?

Action Point: Go to www.hopeforthewearymom.com and down-
load the free *Feel, Know, Do* printable. Print it out and hang it
somewhere where you can see it when you're most likely to lose
your gentle words.

Chapter 7:
When You Want to Run and Hide

Focus Verse: "For the eyes of the Lord move to and fro throughout the earth that He may strongly support those whose heart is completely His" (2 Chronicles 16:9 NASB).

Ice Breaker: What's your favorite color of nail polish? Don't like days at the spa? Share your favorite thing to do to get away for a little while.

Questions for Small Group Discussion

1. How did the definition of *weary* resonate with you?

2. What things do you love to do to relieve stress?

3. How often do you retreat into the comfort of God's Word?

4. Both Mary and Esther ran toward God and the hope he gives. What are some ways you can do the same thing in your daily life?

Action Point: If you don't already have a quiet time routine, commit to creating one. Try getting up just 15 minutes earlier than normal to read a Psalm and a Proverb each day. Ask another mom to hold you accountable.

Chapter 8:
When Life Hurts Too Much

Focus Verse: "Simon Peter answered him, 'Lord, to whom shall we go? You have the words of eternal life, and we have believed, and have come to know that you are the Holy One of God'" (John 6:68-69).

Ice Breaker: Make a prayer box together. Announce this activity at the previous week's session and have everyone bring a small recipe box with index cards. Spend about 15 minutes on this and then let everyone finish at home.

Questions for Small Group Discussion:

1. Have you experienced hard times in the past? Share some of the things you've been through lately...your hurts, losses, or disappointments.

2. It's easy to say we believe God is good and that he always wants our best, but when the difficult times come, the truth of what we really believe often says something totally different. Have you ever experienced a time when you questioned everything you knew to be true about God? Share that experience.

3. If you ever did decide to turn away from Jesus, where would you go?

4. Imagine life without the truth of the Bible. How would it feel to go through life without the love of God and his Word to guide you?

5. Have you decided that Jesus holds the words of eternal life? What does that mean when life doesn't go the way you want it to go?

Action Point: Begin using your prayer box this week. Add to it as the week goes on.

Chapter 9:

When the World Presses In

Focus Verse: "Everyone who comes to me and hears my words and does them, I will show you what he is like: he is like a man building a house, who dug deep and laid the foundation on the rock. And when a flood arose, the stream broke against that house and could not shake it, because it had been well built" (Luke 6:47-48).

Ice Breaker: Talk about the ways the Weary Mom Manifesto from last week's session has impacted the way you see your children this week.

Questions for Small Group Discussion

1. In this chapter, Brooke acknowledges there are moms whose weariness goes beyond the normal day-to-day most of us experience and uses the story of a mom who lost her child in a traumatic way to illustrate her points. But it's important to note that trauma isn't only defined by death. Maybe you had to say goodbye to a dream. Maybe your precious child was born with limitations that make life more challenging for you than others. Or maybe you're raising your children alone. All of these situations fall within the realm of the weariness described in this chapter. Describe the source of your weariness to the group.

2. One of the most important things that helped Tracey as she struggled to stand through the loss of her son was a pre-laid foundation of truth and love in Christ. What's one thing you can do starting today to continue the building process of your faith?

3. Not everyone has the ability, or even desire, to live

in a small town, but we can all have a piece of the "small-town mentality" in the way we open ourselves to relationships. How are you investing in the people God has brought into your life? What's one thing you can begin to do differently that will strengthen your relationships?

4. When we're in the midst of significant trauma, it can be tempting to quit talking to God because we don't trust him as much as we used to. Have you ever walked through a season like this? If so, describe what it felt like.

5. Is it hard or easy for you to see that there's life after loss? Do you find that Tracey's encouragement and personal testimony give you hope for that day to come?

Action Point: Decide what one thing you can begin doing this week to build your faith and take your relationship with God to the next level.

Chapter 10:

Moving from Weariness to Worship

Focus Verse: "...to grant to those who mourn in Zion—to give them a beautiful headdress instead of ashes, the oil of gladness instead of mourning, the garment of praise instead of a faint spirit; that they may be called oaks of righteousness, the planting of the LORD, that he may be glorified" (Isaiah 61:3).

Ice Breaker: What's your favorite hymn or worship song? Explain to the group what the words mean to you and why you love it.

Questions for Small Group Discussion

1. Have you ever just wanted to walk away?

2. Name one way you have left "emotionally" when you are at your most weary.

3. Some people think the only place where you can worship is at church. But that's not true! God, because of Jesus, is available anywhere, anytime to his people! Share some practical everyday places you have worshipped during the craziness of your day (Example: outdoors, alone in the restroom, in bed at night, in front of the Christmas tree, etc.)

4. Name one thing you are grateful for today.

5. What is one way you can create margin in your own life?

Action Point: Think about one area in your life where you can move from weariness to worship (gratitude, margin, find a song to sing). What do you need to do this week to take one step toward Jesus?

Chapter 11:
When You Need HOPE Now

Focus Verse: "May the God of hope fill you with all joy and peace in believing so that by the power of the Holy Spirit you may abound in hope" (Romans 15:13).

Ice Breaker: Which Charlie Brown character do you like most?

Questions for Small Group Discussion

1. Do you ever feel like the older you get, the less organized you become? What do you think contributes to this phenomenon?

2. What does the mess in your heart look like?

3. How does it make you feel to know God cares more about working on your heart than he does changing your circumstances?

4. Does it help you to know that *Hope for the Weary Mom* was written by two moms in the trenches? Not professionals, not moms on the other side of the journey, but moms in the midst of the mess just like you.

5. When was the last time you honestly admitted to God how weary you truly are? How do you think he would handle the news?

Action Point: Copy the prayer in chapter 11, or write your own, pouring out your heart to God.

Resources for the Weary Mom

We've put together a list of wonderful online resources just for you. Take a few minutes and check them out. We pray they will bring you hope.

The Mothers of Daughters Blog:
www.mothersofdaughters.com

The MOB Society blog (for mothers of boys):
www.themobsociety.com

Stacey's Blog: www.staceythacker.com

Brooke's Blog: www.brookemcglothlin.com

Hope for the Weary Mom on Facebook:
www.facebook.com/hopeforthewearymom

The MOD Squad on Facebook:
www.facebook.com/modsquad

The MOB Society on Facebook:
www.facebook.com/themobsociety

Fighting for those Hard-to-Handle Boys:
a five-day challenge from Brooke at
www.prayingforboys.com/challenges

Here's a sneak preview of Brooke and Stacey's next book,
coming August 2015 from Harvest House Publishers

He Is My Rescue

Stacey

*Therefore, say to the people of Israel: "I am the Lord. I will
free you from your oppression and will* **rescue** *you from
your slavery in Egypt. I will redeem you with a powerful
arm and great acts of judgment" (Exodus 6:5-7).*

I imagine there were days when Israel cried out for rescue from the deserts of Egyptian slavery. There must have been times they strained their eyes from looking at the horizon wondering when the rescue was coming. There might also have been days when they forgot the promise and simply went about the backbreaking work without hope.

But God never forgot. From his perspective, he was not late in keeping his promise. He was coming with power and great acts of judgment. He had a plan, and not for one minute did he ever consider doing anything different.

My friend Robin needed a rescue one day. She was walking home from class our senior year at Indiana University during the blizzard of the century. The odds were not in her favor as she set out uphill in the biting, windblown snow toward the apartment we called home.

What she did not know, and I could not tell her in the days before cell phones existed, was that I was making my way toward her.

I had left work early and knew Robin would be getting out of class soon. I knew the way she took and decided I would drive it back to our apartment and pick her up. She was overwhelmed by the storm; all the while I was on a rescue mission. She had no idea rescue was coming, and that was the best part of my plan.

I made my way slowly down the one-way streets in my little red car, straining my eyes to find her. Where was she in this sea of white? Had she taken the bus instead?

Finally in the distance I saw her heavily bundled-up shape trudging slowly through the rapidly falling snow. I was so excited to find her I started blaring my horn. I honked furiously.

Meanwhile, Robin was cold, wet, tired, and possibly a bit cranky. She heard a noise behind her that sounded like an obnoxious driver. I was still some distance away and she had no idea it was me. She grew more annoyed by the moment.

When she finally had enough of my honking, she turned completely around (because let's face it—she had five layers on and could not just turn her head) and saw me for the first time.

The look on her face was priceless. It changed instantly from annoyance to overwhelming joy. She was rescued and she knew it. Even after twenty years, I still remember that day vividly. Rescue is sweet.

There are many days as a mother I remember to cry out for my rescuer to come to me and bring me hope. I remind him of thousands of times he has promised to never leave me. There are just as many days I am buried with making lunches, doing laundry, and loading the dishwasher and I don't. I am like a slave in Israel who has forgotten he always keeps his promises and rescue is coming.

Just like my friend Robin could not see her rescue from my perspective, I can't see from his. He is making his way toward me—all within his perfect timing. He is coming with his eyes deadlocked on me the whole time. When my eyes meet his, overwhelming relief and joy flows.

- He is our rescue.
- He always has been.
- He always will be.
- Even when our weary eyes don't see it coming.

Question: When do you most need a rescue? Do you believe that his promise of rescue is for you as well?

He Prays for You

Brooke

*I do not ask for these only, but also for those who will
believe in me through their word (John 17:20).*

$\mathscr{I}$ made a commitment of faith when I was just nine years old.
Wide-eyed and trembling in the cold baptismal, I nodded my
head in agreement as the pastor of my small Baptist church asked
me if I had decided to give my heart to Jesus. And after it was over,
my mama and a group of sweet church ladies whisked me away to
a Sunday school room to dry me off, get me warm, and make me
presentable. I sat in the pew for the rest of the sermon with wet
hair and a warm heart, because I knew I'd just done something
very important...something that would shape the course of the
rest of my life.

The truth is, I don't remember even one single day where I wasn't
at least aware of God on some level. From the tender age of nine
on (and maybe even before), I've known God had a plan for my
life, believed he was good, and sensed him watching over me. But
in spite of those things—baptism, belief, knowing—I didn't walk
closely with him until I was almost twenty-one years old.

A Dirty Cup

For twelve years I wore the title *Christian* well, but if you'd looked inside my heart you wouldn't have seen much to prove it. I like to call myself a Pharisee, because truly that's what I was. Jesus describes this state of the heart when he's talking to the religious leaders of his time in Matthew 23:25: "Woe to you, scribes and Pharisees, hypocrites! For you clean the outside of the cup and the plate, but inside they are full of greed and self-indulgence."

It's painful to think about, but plain to see that this verse described the way I was living—trying to make my own way while keeping God at arm's length. Knowing his rules and regulations were meant to protect me, but choosing to believe my feelings—what I could see, taste, touch, and hear—rather than the truth of his Word.

It was a recipe for disaster, and one that left me completely vulnerable before the God I had surrendered to as a young girl, and needed to surrender to again.

But as it turns out, my self-built disaster was the best thing that ever happened to me.

I sat on my bed in my college apartment surrounded by reminders of my own attempts to build a kingdom that glorified Brooke, and I wondered how I would find my way back. Ironically (or maybe not so much), I had decided to take a New Testament class that semester, and I remembered I needed to do some reading in the book of John for homework. I picked up my class Bible, turned to John chapter 17, and began to read about the final hours of Jesus's life here on earth.

In verses six through nineteen, Jesus had been praying for his disciples. He knew the struggles they would go through after his death and resurrection, and as his own life hung in the balance, he took the time to cover them in prayer, asking his Father to protect them and lead them well. But verse twenty is different. Look at it closely with me...

"I do not ask for these only, but also for those who will believe in me through their word."

Friend, do you realize who Jesus is talking about in that verse? It's you. It's me. It's every single person who has ever believed based on the testimony of the disciples about the life, death, and resurrection of Jesus. Directly or indirectly, that's every single believer who has ever lived. And Jesus took the time to pray for us before he died.

As I read those words, and the true meaning of them became clear, a new feeling washed over me that drowned out the feelings of despair and hopelessness I had experienced just a few moments before.

Jesus prayed for me.

Me. Within a few hours of that prayer he faced one of the most gruesome deaths ever recorded—a death meant for me, a sacrifice meant to be the punishment for my sins—and instead of worrying about himself, he prayed for me.

And isn't that the real meaning of the cross? That God's love for us was so great, his devotion to us so sincere, that he sent his one and only Son to die on the cross and take the punishment for our sins? He's all about love—a love so great that it's more concerned with the object of its desire (you and me) even in the face of great pain and trial, humiliation, wrongful accusation, and death.

Today, let that kind of love wash over you like it did for me that day in my apartment, now over fifteen years ago. In your darkest days, the ones where you're tempted to despair and wonder if God truly hears you, truly sees you, remember that he prayed for you, and according to scripture, still does (Hebrews 7:25).

Question: Most people pray for others because they care about what happens to them. How does it make you feel to know Jesus cared enough for you to pray for your well-being?

Want to see more from Brooke and Stacey?
Check out their most beloved blog posts!

Stacey
Dear Weary Mom

Dear Weary Mom,
I am so glad you are here.

I know what it might have taken for you to wander by this way and it is no small thing. You may be hiding in the bathroom with your smartphone or up late feeding the baby. Maybe you are in a car line waiting for the kids to be released from school for the holiday. As a weary mom, we know you are multitasking right this very minute.

I've been thinking about you and praying for you. If you were here in real life, I'd ask you to sit at my table and probably apologize for the dishes in the sink. You would of course be gracious and say, "It makes me feel at home." I would pretend I meant to do that for you. I'd rustle up some coffee for us and we'd get right down to a chat about life and kids and how much we love Target.

Our stories would connect because we are moms. We know what it is like to have our hearts walking around outside our bodies while being so tired we'd pay a total stranger large amounts of money to let us sleep for six hours straight. *Weary moms get each other.*

In the end, we would talk about Jesus and I'd ask to pray over you and tell you that we are going to make it because we do not walk alone. We can lay our burdens down right here on the Word made flesh and we can ask for His strength to be made be perfect in our weak places.

A mama needs to go. She needs to remember before she was a mama she was a girl who could carry on adult conversations and eat an entire meal without being interrupted. Guilt will try to keep her from remembering and fear will tell her she'd be better off staying. But unless she finds bread for herself, she will not have anything left to give others. *And truth be told, they will thank her for going in the end.*

A mama needs to laugh. She needs to laugh long and loud and not apologize for it. She may need to laugh about being a mother or something funny her kids said. But it's perfectly okay to laugh at hilarious lines from a movie too. *Laughing lets go of the stress and frees her up to receive.*

A mama needs to dream. A mama who dreams will raise babies who dream. She needs to realize that her dreams matter to God because they started with Him. *If she gives them to Him and listens real close, He'll give them wings.*

A mama needs friends who cheer her on. She needs to be able to kick her shoes off and talk long with a sweet sister over pizza and swap stories. A mama's heart grows ten times bigger when another mama looks at her and says, *"I believe in what God is doing here."*

A mama needs to worship. She needs to be reminded that God is bigger and deeper than anything four kids can dish out. *She needs to raise her hands and release her smallness into the arms of a graceful Father who loves to love her through song.*

A mama needs a challenging word. The mission we call motherhood is not for the faint of heart, and the only thing that will get us through is the Word made flesh Himself. His Words bring courage. His Words also shed light on the dark places. *And a challenge well spoken will rally us to the frontline willingly.*

A mama needs to return. She needs to hear her children squeal with delight when she exits the taxi and feel the warmth of their breath on her neck as they squeeze her so tight she can't breathe. *She* *also needs to realize that they survived without her for a few days, and as good as it is to be home, it was certainly okay to leave.*

God-Sized-Dream Girl

I see you standing there. You are wondering how in the world your dream will fly when you can't seem to get the pile of laundry off the dining room table. You are thinking to yourself, *"I am crazy to believe my dream matters."*

But I want to tell you it does. Your dream matters. It matters for two reasons you can't argue with.

First of all, the dream you have in your heart was put there by the One who knows you best. He knows your ways. He knows your gifts and your abilities. He is not bothered one bit by the laundry kicking your tail. *His plans for you are good,* and he doesn't waste time on dreams that don't matter.

And your dream matters because God flat out loves you, girl. What you care about—well, He cares about. He wants to see you shine like the stars for him. Your God-sized dream is not about you. It is all about his glory. You get to be part of it because he loves you and wants to see you wrapped up in it doing what he created you to do. This will bring you great joy. His glory and your joy is a winning combination.

I know if you had a day like I had today, you might be tempted to think, *Why bother?* Why say it, share it, make it, do it, or pursue anything that remotely looks like a God-sized dream? *Some days feel dreadfully ordinary.* But in these ordinary days, God is making you like himself. He is at work behind the scenes to prepare the time and place for your dream to take flight.

And in his timing it will fly, dream girl. You will be so glad you didn't miss one breathtaking moment of the journey.

Even the ordinary laundry-filled days like today.

Brooke
What Is an Extraordinary Life?

What does it take to go from ordinary to extraordinary? How does a life go from boring to beautiful? What does it require to live a life in passionate pursuit of God, His plan, His purpose?

There seems to be a push among Christians to "do something big" for the kingdom of God. Rightfully so—with children starving, women being raped, babies being forcefully aborted, and families drinking sludge instead of clean water.

Clearly, there is much work—good work—to be done, and I'm not against any of it. My family is passionate about supporting our local Crisis Pregnancy Center, the MOB Society is gearing up to support a missionary through Wycliffe Bible Translators, and I give my time and words as often as I can to those without the Bible in their own heart language as a support to the Seed Company.

All of these are good, necessary, worthwhile things. They're real. The people they serve are real. The needs are real. Some of the situations are desperate—life and death—and require deep personal sacrifice to make even the smallest of changes.

I admit, as I've read the stories of the people whose very lives are changed through these ministries—some coming to know Christ for the first time—I've been moved to action. I've watched as women I admire travel abroad, bringing attention to those who need our care and love and money so very much, and thought, "That must be what it's like to live an extraordinary life!" Traveling, seeing, spreading the word so others can get involved.

I've listened as Christian writers and speakers passionately share the Word of God in front of thousands, changing the lives of countless people for the better, and thought, "That must be what it's like to live an extraordinary life!" Studying, training, offering pure hearts so that others can know the truth.

A life that really matters. A life that's truly beautiful. A life spent for God's glory. Those things…*they* must be what it looks like to live an extraordinary life.

And yet…

And yet as a mom—just a simple, stay-at-home mama—who works from her office that doubles as a homeschool room, and who has to move that plastic globe (the one she uses most weeks to teach her boys that the world is much bigger than what they can see) hanging from the window out of the way so you can't see it on a home-grown video—I sometimes look at these world-changers and am tempted to think my own efforts fall sadly short of the extraordinary.

The mom who says, "love others more than you love yourself" for the hundredth time in one day…

Who does the dishwasher for the second time in 24 hours…

Who struggles just to find a second to wash her hair…

Who puts the work that means the world to her on hold because that little one needs to hear he's loved one more time…

Who prays and prays and begs God to move in something so very small, and notices He seems to be interested in bigger things…

Who asks God daily to give her joy in the mundane, to keep her from losing her mind as siblings fight over nothing AGAIN…

Her life can feel a little like that plastic globe hanging from the window, with a glimpse of the most extraordinary things so far away—the things yet to be seen, yet to be fixed—and the ordinary staring her in the face, leaving her feeling like her contribution to the world isn't all that important.

And I wonder when motherhood lost its extraordinary.

Not that the people in foreign lands, or even right down the street, don't need someone to come to them in Jesus's name, but that the people right under our noses, and all the sacrifice required to love them well, need us just as much.

When did encouraging women to "love their husbands and children, be self-controlled, pure, working at home, kind, and submissive to their own husbands…" become passé? When did we stop believing that a call to motherhood, loving one man, service in our homes, and sacrifice for the sake of raising godly children was truly extraordinary? When did we start believing that there had to be something more, something bigger, something more important to qualify us for the extraordinary?

Motherhood is often unseen. Unnoticed. And the change it evokes in the lives of generations upon generations—while having the potential to impact the kingdom in untold deep and profound ways—is slow, tedious, and requires diligence and patience and sacrifice…day, after day, after day. There's no glory in the calling to bring forth life until that child rises up and calls us blessed…IF that child rises up and calls us blessed.

But I say it requires an even greater degree of faith to stare down deep into the eyes of the ordinary and call it extraordinary.

Not that our command to "go therefore, and preach the Gospel to all nations" shouldn't cause some of us to physically go. It should, and it will, and there will be big sacrifices required of some to obey the call. But going to the nations should include the little heathens at home.

Here, in the throes of dirty diapers, runny noses, selfish hearts, bratty brothers, and sinful, slothful, needy, sometimes unloving children. Here, in the throes of sometimes thankless marriages. Here, in the throes of important callings that play second fiddle to that which is even more important—loving our families well. Extraordinary *here*, regardless of what's happening *there*.

Mama, your life—with all its ups and downs, starts and stops, victories and defeats, praises and heartbreaks—is extraordinary. You don't need to add anything else to your to-do list to be beautiful. You can passionately pursue God, his plan, and his purpose right where you are with the people group who need to hear the gospel from you most.

All the little ways you serve, sacrifice, believe, pray, share, and love…all added up together make you extraordinary. You are nothing short of extraordinary, and God says that's enough. I'm reclaiming the word "extraordinary" for simple, every day, run of the mill motherhood. You with me?

Here's the Thing About Fighting for Your Children

The one thing I don't want you to think is that I have it all together.

Mostly, I'm a complete and utter mess…a mom, just like you, trying to keep her head above water in a crazy world that wants to take everything I have to offer.

I run out of time. I run out of patience. I run out of toilet paper. I run out of money. I run out of me. (In other words, there's not enough of me to go around.) Some days I just want to give up, leave it all to chance, and hope things turn out okay. But several months ago, in a time of deep and intense prayer, God made it clear to me that my boys needed someone to fight for them, and that that person needed to be me.

So I'm fighting.

I don't always get it right, and sometimes I think I'm doing it all wrong. But I'm fighting. I'm giving this battle for their hearts everything I have, and trusting God to take care of the rest.

But these things we're fighting for, they don't happen overnight. I wish they did. I wish when I looked my sons in the eyes—nose-to-nose and heart-to-heart—and shared the secrets to life, they would take root and produce fruit right away. Most of the time, they don't. Just today, my oldest let his emotions get away from him. By God's grace, I recognized it as an opportunity to reach for his heart, so I got down on his level, pulled him onto my lap, and asked, "Son, where do we go to find the truth?"

His reply? "The Bible."

"That's right, Son," I said, "we go to the Bible to find truth. It helps us to know the difference between right and wrong. Just now, you felt justified in acting the way you did, because you thought you were right. But the Bible tells us your response was very wrong. So if we think one thing is right, but the Bible says something different, who do we believe?"

He looked down a little, and said, "The Bible."

"That's right!" his happy mama said. "So if we feel we're right, but the Bible says we're wrong, who needs to change?"

"We do," he said, and I hugged him tight, whispering in his ear, "Hang on to that, Son. It will serve you well all your life."

I left that conversation feeling great. But you know what? (I bet you can guess...) Later this afternoon, we dealt with the same thing all over again.

I used to feel like a total failure when these things happened, because surely if I mess up I'm a bad mom, and surely my kid is going to struggle with that issue for the rest of his life, right?

Wrong. Raising good, respectable (and hopefully) godly children takes time. If we mess up there's new mercy for tomorrow, and certain struggles do get outgrown with time. But only a new day can make us believe it. Only the gift of time and perspective gives a mom hope to believe things will change and strength to keep moving her feet toward that day.

Faith is believing that what we can't see will be. Why? Because God's Word never returns void, and the heart of a fighting mama is a heart that pleases God.

So we keep fighting. Keep hoping. Keep reaching for their hearts. Keep offering all this as a gift to God...our way of serving him and making his name great with our own lives.

Notes

Introduction

1. MG Siegler, "Steve Jobs Resigns as CEO of Apple," Technocrunch (blog), August 24, 2011, http://techcrunch.com/2011/08/24/steve-jobs-resigns-from-apple/.

2. Stacey Thacker, "Steve Jobs, Me, and Being Fresh Out of Amazing", 29 Lincoln Avenue (blog), August 25, 2011, http://www.29lincolnavenue.com/2011/08/steve-jobs-me-and-being -fresh-out-of-amazing/.

Chapter 2: When You're Caught in What You're Not

1. Susan Cain, *Quiet: The Power of Introverts in a World That Can't Stop Talking* (Crown Publishing, 2013), 11.

Chapter 3: Confronting Carol

1. A.W. Tozer, *The Pursuit of God* (Camp Hill, PA: Christian Publications, Inc., 1993), 44.

2. C.S. Lewis, *The Four Loves* (New York: Harcourt, Brace, 1960), 78.

3. Emily P. Freeman, *Grace for the Good Girl* (Grand Rapids, MI: Revell, 2011), 14.

Chapter 4: The Marathon of Mothering

1. Derek M.Hansen, "Where You Look Can Affect How You Look: Running Mechanics and Gaze Control," August 4, 2009, http://www.runningmechanics.com/articles/biomechanics -and-technique/where-you-look-can-affect-how-you-look-running-mechanics-and-gaze-con trol/.

Chapter 5: Redeeming Mommy Guilt

1. Archie & Peyton Manning with John Underwood, *Manning: A Father, His Sons, and a Football Legacy* (New York: Harper Collins Publishers, 2010), 363.

2. Lysa Terkeurst, *Unglued* (Grand Rapids, MI: Zondervan, 2012), 98.

Chapter 6: When Gentle Words Won't Come

1. Excerpted from: Brooke McGlothlin, *How to Control Your Emotions So They Don't Control You*, ebook, 2013.

Chapter 7: When You Want to Run and Hide

1. Studylight, s.v. "Weary", accessed January 20, 2013, Studylight.org, http://www.studylight.org/ lex/heb/hwview.cgi?n=5774.

Chapter 8: When Life Hurts Too Much

1. Matthew Henry, *Matthew Henry Commentary on the Whole Bible (Complete)*, "John 11," http://www.biblestudytools.com/commentaries/matthew-henry-complete/john/11.html.

Chapter 10: Moving from Weariness to Worship

1. Koa Bec, "All the Single Daddies: More than Ever Raising Families," April 27, 2012, http://www.mommyish.com/2012/04/27/single-fathers-statistics-2012.

2. Colleen Moore, quoted in Rachel Mosteller, "Why Moms Are At Risk for Internet Addiction," April 28, 2009, http://www.cnn.com/2009/HEALTH/04/13/mothers.internet.addiction.

3. Priscilla Shirer, lecture at the Going Beyond Conference, Orlando, FL, May 2012.

4. Helen H. Lemmel, "Turn Your Eyes Upon Jesus," 1922.

5. Ann Voskamp, "Joy Dares," *A Holy Experience* (blog), http://www.aholyexperience.com/joy-dares/.

6. Hannah Hurnard, *Hinds Feet on High Places* (London: Christian Literature Crusade, 1955), 90.

Chapter 11: When You Need HOPE Now

1. Milton Vincent, *A Gospel Primer for Christians* (Bemidji, MN: Focus Publishing, 2008), 14.

About the Authors

Stacey Thacker:

Stacey is wife to Mike and the mother of four vibrant girls. She is a writer and speaker who loves God's Word and a good cup of coffee. Her passion is to connect with women and encourage them in their walks with God. Stacey is the owner of Mothers of Daughters, a blog for modern moms wanting to raise girls with timeless truth and vintage values, and the author of *Being OK with Where You Are*. You can find her blogging at www.staceythacker.com or hanging out on Twitter @staceythacker.

Brooke McGlothlin:

Brooke is cofounder of Raising Boys Ministries, where moms and dads come to discover delight in the chaos of raising boys. You can find her writing about fighting for the hearts of her sons at the MOB Society blog or living a life in pursuit of Jesus at her personal blog, www.brookemcglothlin.com. She's the author of *Praying for Boys: Asking God for the Things They Need Most*, and other books for moms.

A normal day finds Brooke homeschooling her two boys, wrangling two large Labs, Toby and Siri, writing to bring hope to the messes of life (in the midst of her own messy life), and falling more and more in love with the man she's had a crush on since the third grade (who just happens to be her husband).

CHOOSE HOPE

Join the *Hope for the Weary Mom* community
by scanning the code above with your smartphone.